Life
in
Babylon

A Memoir of Joy and Anguish

Theresa M. Santmann

also known as
Theresa Patnode

LIFE IN BABYLON
A MEMOIR OF JOY AND ANGUISH

iUniverse books may be ordered through booksellers or by contacting:

iUniverse
1663 Liberty Drive
Bloomington, IN 47403
www.iuniverse.com
1-800-Authors (1-800-288-4677)

ISBN: 978-1-4917-4249-5 (sc)
ISBN: 978-1-4917-4251-8 (hc)
ISBN: 978-1-4917-4250-1 (e)

Library of Congress Control Number: 2014913502

Printed in the United States of America.

iUniverse rev. date: 10/09/2014

To Raymond Patnode, my brother, who
has been unceasingly supportive
through good times and bad times. I love him.

And to my good friend Philip Simone
who made this book come to be.

Contents

Prologue ix

Chapter 1   Theresa M. Santmann History 1

Chapter 2   Moving On...7

Chapter 3   The Manhattan Apartment 11

Chapter 4   Wanting a Second Child 21

Chapter 5   We Had to Make a Change 25

Chapter 6   Wicky One, 1963 31

Chapter 7   Building Little Flower Nursing Home.....................37

Chapter 8   Solo Cross-Country 41

Chapter 9   A Son Leaves Home 45

Chapter 10 Jack Santmann Hospitalization...............................49

Chapter 11 Struggling...59

Chapter 12 Little Flower Nursing Home: 1971–1975 61

Chapter 13 Words to Disabled Husband Jack 65

Chapter 14 Jack Santmann...67

Chapter 15 Attacks...71

Chapter 16 Coming to Terms with Death 77

Chapter 17 Death Watch 81

Chapter 18 I Miss Him...83

Chapter 19 Mother and Daughter..85

Chapter 20 Thoughts on Life and Death 91

Chapter 21 Served a Subpoena at Little Flower Nursing Home ...95

Chapter 22 A Daughter Leaves Home 97

Chapter 23 Visiting Five Russian Hospitals, 1979 99

Chapter 24 Building a Second Nursing Home 151
Chapter 25 Traveling with Nanna 157
Chapter 26 Thanksgiving with Nanna 161
Chapter 27 Babylon Village Republican Club Western
           Barbecue 165
Chapter 28 Submarine USS *Oklahoma City* 169
Chapter 29 On the Town 173
Chapter 30 Road to Adelaide, Australia 177
Chapter 31 Wearing Out of Angel Wings 181
Chapter 32 Musing, Dad Samuel Patnode, and Others 185
Chapter 33 Around the World 189
Chapter 34 Amboseli National Park, Africa 193
Chapter 35 Yamal (Nuclear-Powered Russian Icebreaker) 197
Chapter 36 The Little Flower Residence: Rescinding Operating
           Certificate 203
Chapter 37 Memories 207
Chapter 38 A Life Filled With Wonderful Memories 212
Chapter 39 Odds and Ends 225
Chapter 40 Keep Me in a Pocket Next to Your Heart 249

Prologue

My parents, of French Canadian ancestry, brought their Catholic backgrounds much into evidence in raising their eight girls and four boys. I was the fifth child. There was great parental disappointment that none of the children followed the example of my mother's four aunts at a convent in Saint Mary's, Pennsylvania.

The cultural differences between country life on a farm and the city life I was to adapt at a later period cannot be overemphasized.

For what later seems so trivial and only the minutia of life, a mental frame of reference needed to be established for myself if I was ever to meet my goals as I moved into the cosmopolitan arena of business and society.

I think that people might assume that I had a rather energetic work ethic along with a strong drive to have arrived at a later period in my life ensconced by myself in a large house with a Doberman and a little poodle, with the means to live comfortably.

I have met many people who have knowingly, or maybe unknowingly, been supportive of me and have helped me along the road of life.

I am grateful to be living and in comparatively good health.

Writing a book about my life has given me a measure of contentment that maybe I am leaving a bit of myself that will be thought of in a positive and encouraging light. Mental imagery might be important or at least helpful for people struggling to better the accident of their birth. After all, when changing a familial position in life it is necessary to have a positive frame of reference for oneself.

John Santmann Jr. and
Theresa A. Santmann posing in
front of the residents of the
Little Flower Residence seated
in lawn chairs, 1962.

Chapter 1

Theresa M. Santmann History

I was born in the Sam Patnode family homestead in Ellenburg Center. The dairy farm is located in northern New York State at the foot of the Adirondack Mountains near the Canadian border. My family eked out an existence from the rock-filled soil. Everyday life was filled with a wide range of experiences, from the moving sight of a calf struggling to its feet in its first moments of life to the constant battle against nature's vicissitudes, such as the herd decimated by mastitis and bitterly cold winters coupled with searing poverty. The North Country offered almost no chances for improvement or advancement out of the circumstances into which someone was born.

I had just finished a postgraduate year in a high school near Fort Jackson, New York, where my family had moved to after a fire burned our Ellenburg Center barn to the ground. Where was I to go with no money? My mother found out about a job opening at McManus's Restaurant in Potsdam, New York. I went with her to the restaurant. She quizzed the owner at length, trying to make absolutely sure that I would not be serving any alcoholic beverages in the dining area where I would be working. I was mortified by her insistent questioning. I got the job despite her abrupt manner.

I had been working at the restaurant for several months, when parents' weekend was coming up. Another restaurant in the village offered me a little more money and assured me security for ongoing employment. Being unfamiliar with the practice of many businesspeople, I took the job. As soon as the weekend festivities passed, I was fired. Somehow with homemade bread and eating out with boyfriends, I was able to accept a very kind suggestion from the dean of Potsdam State Teachers College to take several college courses for the last half of the school year.

During this time period, I met an engineering student named Robert Jervis, who was attending Clarkson College in Potsdam. His home was in Maple Shade, New Jersey. He offered to have me move in with his sister, who lived near his parents. I took him up on the offer, and, with eighteen dollars in my pocket, I moved in with his sister. I found a job in the Laundromat where Robert's mother worked, folding linens. My next endeavor was working for a publishing company in Philadelphia. After that came RCA in Camden, New Jersey. My salary was forty-two dollars a week as a statistical clerk in the corporate wage and salary division.

While working at RCA, I joined a newly formed girls' basketball team. RCA originally had a girls' basketball team made up of factory employees. We were told they were so rough that they were giving RCA a bad name, so the team was disbanded and a team of office personnel was established. I loved playing basketball. One year our team was in the play-offs in New York City. I would play so hard that I would turn a deep red, with perspiration running down my face. Whenever there was a rough woman on the other team, I would invariably be the one to guard her.

I had a party at my apartment for the RCA girls' basketball team and their dates. That's where I first met my future husband, John Santmann. The name Jack was frequently used in lieu of his official name of John. Jack had a friend named Raymond Linder. They were college buddies of long standing. As the friendship between Jack and me intensified, Ray became very agitated and finally talked Jack into ending our relationship.

Days went by without hearing from Jack. I had a vacation coming up. This was a good time to visit my parents in Fort Jackson, New York. The visit was for two weeks. Jack somehow found out the approximate date of my return. He parked his car on the street by my apartment and waited through the night for my return. After that we saw each other every day for a few months as his friendship with Ray Linder grew more distant. Soon we were married.

Jack and I each brought debts to our marriage. I was still paying off my first two pieces of furniture, a gray two-piece sectional and a green sofa bed. Many years later they were used when we started the Little Flower Residence, an adult home. Jack's car was a secondhand Studebaker. Between his car and the tuition he was still paying off for a bachelor's degree from Temple University, he also had some debts. After our wedding, I continued working for RCA. Jack worked as an insurance salesman. He hated the job. When I was not working, I went with him and waited in the car as he made house calls. Soon I was pregnant and anticipating the completion of my very own family. Within the next year we brought our son, John, home from the hospital. We lived in an attached single-family house in Philadelphia, Pennsylvania.

John's delivery had been difficult, with his birth weight at 9 pounds, 10.5 ounces. Forceps had done a number on his skull. John's head had such difficulty passing through the birth canal that his head resembled a football, as a result. Even though I had started breastfeeding him the day after the delivery, on the second day he wasn't brought to my room, while other babies were brought to their mothers. Soon a group of people consisting of a priest, my pediatrician, a nurse, and several others came into my room and approached my bed. They had come to tell me that my son, John, was bleeding under the skull and that he had been baptized first by a nurse many hours before and then again by a priest. He was not expected to live.

Words are inadequate in describing the few days that followed. Babies arrived and went to other mothers as I kept pumping my breasts in an effort to feed my far-away baby. I was asked if my extra breast milk could go to other preemies in the nursery. The answer was yes, even as I scanned every face coming in the room for the dreadful signs of a possible death. Finally, baby John came back to my bedside.

Jack and I took our delightful son, John, back to our 1.5-room apartment. John was such a treasure. On his second day home, I forgot about the caution needed in changing a boy's diaper. I was changing him on the bed. His little urine stream hit my nose. Jack and I lay back on the bed, convulsing with laughter. When John was three months old, we traveled to the Jersey shore to see a whale that had been washed up on the beach, even though Jack had to go to work the next day. The whale's eyes looked like specks on its huge gray sides. The inside of its gaping mouth had long, hanging sheets that looked as if they did exactly what was written in books about sucking in seawater and straining out their food by then blowing out the seawater. I breastfed John sitting on a park bench. Next we went on a merry-go-round before starting our long trip home.

John was a wonderful, incredibly physical child. At only eight months old he started climbing out of his crib. With each escape we lowered the mattress till finally it was hanging by wires. His crib was placed so that he could stand at the end of the crib and peer into our room. One time I thought maybe it would help if his crib was placed so he couldn't peer into our room. Maybe he would go back to sleep. It was not to be. It was early in the morning and about time for his peekaboo. He started to cry. I thought maybe he would cry, get tired, and go back to sleep. I was not accustomed to that precious baby crying. I was about to get John out of his crib when the cries seemed to be getting closer and softer. There he was coming through the doorway, dragging his blanket along. I cried with him while giving him hugs. The landlord, even in very cold weather, seldom turned the heat on in our building. We tried unscrewing the valves of the radiators only to find out there was to be no heat no matter what we did. We filled the bathtub with water as warm as it would come out of the faucet, covered John's crib with a blanket and left the stove on even when it wasn't being used. No matter what we did, the apartment was never comfortable. Soon after John was born, we moved to a two-family house in the suburbs of Philadelphia.

John was such a bundle of joy. His escapades were done with such glee. After just unrolling a whole roll of toilet paper all over the bathroom floor, he came out laughing. He threw a teddy bear named Sputnik out of our car window while we were driving on a three-lane highway north of the city. The teddy bear was named after the first space vehicle. John was crying, as if his heart was broken. Finally, he understood we were going back to the site of his mischief. It was many extra miles, but we were able to retrieve the little bear. When the first Sputnik wore out, I carefully undid its seams and made Sputnik number two and then later number three from its parts.

John's first birthday party still holds a special place in my heart. Several neighborhood girls thought he was cute. About eight children of different ages attended the party. Through all the festivities John ran from one end of the house to the other, squealing with glee as his proud parents looked on. Jack and I both loved John's little red wagon. I dressed him in his red toque and bulky red sweater, and we paraded down the sidewalk in front of our house.

John Santmann and Theresa Patnode wedding picture, 1954.

Chapter 2

Moving On

There were very few jobs available for a psychology major. We were very anxious for Jack to get a PhD in experimental psychology. He submitted a number of applications to different universities offering such degrees. At last, our most ambitious dream came true. Jack was accepted at Columbia University. His stipend was a mere two thousand dollars. In addition, they discouraged any other endeavors while enrolled. We had a little over one month to leave our cozy house in Philadelphia for the big city of New York.

Next came a period of scrambling, trying to find an acceptable place to live with low rent in Manhattan. Jack had gone ahead of me and had started working at one of the two jobs he had managed to get.

A paper strike in Philadelphia was such a blessing because the landlord couldn't advertise, so we were allowed to stay on a day-to-day basis. We agreed Jack would rent a room until we could find an apartment. We left the furniture in the Philadelphia house and moved to the only place that became available rather quickly; it was a furnished room. I had packed a few boxes with canned products, potatoes, pots and pans, linens, etc. I hadn't seen the room before carrying the first box in, and I quickly placed it on the floor. I didn't hesitate in helping to carry in more boxes. I covered all the dingy, worn, and slightly soiled furniture with white sheets. I cleaned the closets, hot plate, and small sink.

I had dealt with cockroaches in our Philadelphia house, where their only place of residence was the basement's gray-painted cement floor. They were almost friendly. They were the size of an elongated silver dollar and quite black. They moved slowly enough for me to win the battle in a chase. In addition, they could not climb walls, so the war was rather one-sided in my favor.

By the time everything was unloaded, we were very hungry. It was time to get some food out of the brown cardboard boxes on the floor. I opened a box, and, much to my horror, an army of brown roaches came pouring out. I had never seen a brown roach. They were smaller and much faster than their Philadelphia cousins. They infested all the food that wasn't canned. They climbed walls. I was to learn that in Manhattan, at least in our one room and where we eventually moved to on Riverside Drive, battling roaches was a way of life.

Jack and Theresa Santmann in their New York City apartment, celebrating son John's birthday with neighbors' children, 1957.

Chapter 3

The Manhattan Apartment

Our Manhattan apartment came about in a last-minute, desperate way. Every time Jack and I went to look at apartments, there seemed to be in plain sight a tablet with names next to dollar amounts. After a few viewings, we finally figured it out. People vying for apartments were volunteering an under-the-table cash payment. The amounts that had been bid were left for the next prospective tenant to see as the landlord tried to get a higher bid than the ones we were looking at. There was a voluntary bidding war taking place. In each instance there was no way we could match or beat the amounts that were already on the table. There was one hope. We knew that there were quite a few rent-controlled apartments in Manhattan. If an apartment ad was in the Sunday paper and was reasonably priced and we were the first callers we might have a chance. After all, Jack was a PhD candidate, so the chances were good that we would not be semipermanent Manhattan residents. With a rent-controlled apartment, an increase in rent could be charged only with every new tenant.

There was an advertisement for an apartment in the Sunday newspaper. Calls for the apartment almost certainly would not be answered till Monday morning at 9:00 a.m. Jack went to a phone booth and started phoning at 8:40 a.m. and just kept redialing. Sure enough, we were the first callers. Jack and I went to see the rental agent. We made our paltry bid of two hundred dollars, which we certainly could not afford. We were kept waiting for several days until finally we heard the answer we so desperately needed to hear. The apartment was ours. Jack had already started his Brooklyn job by the time the apartment was to be ours.

After finally securing the apartment, there were many problems that needed immediate attention. How were we to move the furniture from the Philadelphia house to our new apartment as cheaply as humanly possible? In addition, Jack needed to start his new job immediately. The apartment was on the third floor and desperately needed scrubbing, cleaning, and painting. We hired the least expensive moving company we could find. The belongings from our New York one-room had already been moved to our new apartment.

It was early morning, and daylight was just breaking over the horizon. Jack had gone off to work at his guard job at the Brooklyn House of Detention. I was alone in the apartment with two-year-old John and still curious about my new surroundings. I happened to look out of the window and noticed that on the street three floors below was a truck. It was a rather decrepit one that had several men milling around the back of it. Several other men had just let down the tailgate. I thought, *Oh my God, that is our furniture that just arrived!* The man milling about was obviously not there just to help unload the furniture. I was screaming down at him to go away and that was my furniture coming off the truck. He barely glanced up. I couldn't leave John, and I knew even if I took him with me it certainly wouldn't be safe for us. Just then a police car moved down the street and stopped to find out what was going on. I could hear the man in the street say he had been asked to help move the furniture. I was terrified and screamed, "That's not true. He is only trying to steal!" I hurried down to the street with baby John to explain what was happening. Those wonderful police said, "Don't worry. He won't bother you again."

The apartment's living room overlooked the Hudson River. Off in the distance were the magnificent rising arches of the George Washington Bridge, with television's Captain Kangaroo's Little Red Lighthouse tucked under its embracing arms. As two-year-old John was already a Captain Kangaroo fan, we were fascinated with the lighthouse. The living room opened to the dining room, which served as baby John's bedroom with its bunk beds. The three-and-a-half-foot-wide hallway went from the dining room, past the small kitchen, to the bath, then the bedroom, and finally stretched another thirty feet to the front door of the apartment. As soon as the door was opened, the pungent odor of garlic permeated the area. Past the door to our apartment was a stairway and an elevator.

We had been in the apartment for a day or two when I started smelling a rather disagreeable odor. I had never lived in Manhattan and had only visited the city several times. Maybe the smell was coming off the Hudson River or from trash pickup. From day one there was the ever-present, stale smell of garlic, but this was in addition to the garlic. It was approximately ten days later, and the smell became increasingly pungent and incredibly disagreeable. There was commotion in the hall. I went out to investigate. A city cop was in the hall, and the door to the apartment on my left was open. The cop turned toward me and tried to quickly shoo me back into my apartment. I asked him what was going on. Someone had died. That was where the smell came from, the dead body. I caught a glimpse of a discolored body and then hurriedly went back into my apartment.

The two years in our New York City apartment were filled with very different highlights. An old man had lived by himself in the apartment for many years. There was a stove that came alive with brown roaches when lit. A dining-room floor that had beautiful hardwood twelve inch square which only became visible with two buckets of water, cleaning compounds, and a scrub brush for each square foot before the intricate design could be seen.

I was determined to keep the roaches out and kill the ones that had been housed there for so many years. No matter how much cleaning, scrubbing, and chemical warfare I used, they held firm to the outskirts of the oven walls. Only the heat of the burners or the oven made them scamper away for other housing. The high glass shelf on the other wall was used for canned goods. Surely the little devils would have a hard time at best getting up to that shelf, but alas I lifted a large can of fruit juice and a whole family, large and small, came pouring out. One time I was heating water in a teakettle. As I poured out the water I saw they were tiny and colorless. I supposed that was their color before they were exposed to light.

We finally got a washing machine, which had no place to go but the kitchen. Of course, no matter what I did, roaches always found another home. Several years later when we moved on to our Westbury, Long Island, home, we tried to leave all of our unwelcome guests in the city. The washing machine carried enough of them that there was a shorter, but no less intense, six-month war. I would get up during the night and make my way to a darkened kitchen, roach spray can at the ready. Turning on the light and running after them finally led to victory.

Our New York apartment had another point of concern, a dumbwaiter. No amount of spackle could possibly do the entire job. First I used wads of paper stuffed into anything that provided an opening to the kitchen before applying a layer of spackle. It took me over four months of scraping and thirty pounds of spackle to try to get all the holes and cracks in the kitchen area sealed, the apartment floors scrubbed, and the walls sanded and painted in mostly pale pastels. I was honing my skills in sanding and spackling. It would come in handy when I started the Little Flower Residence in 1961 and had to be a jack-of-all-trades. Our living room furniture came from my long-ago single days in my one-room Maple Shade, New Jersey, apartment. There was a gray sectional sofa, a dark-green sofa bed, and a green carpet.

Another memory of our son, John, getting into mischief was when I was painting the bedroom. I was using paint by the gallon, to which I added tubes of coloring to get the exact color I wanted. He had taken a tube of coloring and somehow had managed to make a connection in a light socket that melted the tiny metal cap on the tube. He was screaming while running the length of the room with the tube in his hand, and it was leaving a trail of coloring in its wake. He seemed to have no ill effects from the shock he must have gotten. Jack and I dragged the rug to the tub in the bathroom and worked for hours trying to undo the staining. The running water did little to help our repair efforts.

The bedroom was finished in a pale pink. Although the kitchen was many feet away from our bedroom, on occasion a roach would awaken me, and I would scream as it scurried across my arm. It was a rather large, comfortable room compared to the other rooms. It had two south-facing windows looking out at another apartment building across the street. A fire escape wended its way past the easterly window. Despite some misgivings, we had nailed it shut. The general area, at least when we first moved to the city, did not lend itself to a feeling of security.

I painted three walls of the living room in green and the fourth wall a rust color. Baby John's room had not only French doors to the living room but lovely bay windows. I painted the room a pale lavender. The room carried a number of memories besides its scrubbed twelve-inch squares. There were no storm windows, so wind coming off the Hudson River through the living-room's west-facing windows found its whining strength turn to almost mystical proportions as it pushed the inside French doors into an open position. Wedging the doors closed with material and trying to find something with enough weight to load against the doors was a never-ending trial in the blustery days of winter. The long hall in the apartment got the last treatment and took the longest. I had been having a battle over paint with the landlord. He wanted me to use whitewash. We had used that color a year back in the barns at my family's Ellenburg Center farm. My argument was that I was doing all the work and the least he could do was to give me real paint. Of course I had to get the cheapest grade of paint and then had to put on at least two coats of paint to cover the walls. The hall had an incredible amount of peeling paint. I counted forty buckets of paint chips before I finished that job.

I did all of our laundry, which included baby John's diapers. I strung clotheslines the length of the long hall. A knock came at the door. It was an insurance salesman I forgot was coming. There I was, leading him down the narrow hall between two rows of clothesline and John's newly used potty to our little kitchen to discuss business. Oh well. Usually I was neater than that.

One night my angel paid a visit. Baby John had been given a train set that we had set up next to his bed. Inadvertently he had left it in the on position. I was awoken in the middle of the night. Our bedroom was many feet away from John's room. I trotted down the hall, and for only the slightest moment I stood transfixed. Rising from the train's transformer was a curl of smoke with the distinctive smell of an electrical fire. It was so close to a horrid tragedy.

Our apartment was on 138th Street, with one of the windows in the living room facing south on Riverside Drive. When Jack came home from his nighttime job as a part-time psychologist at the Brooklyn House of Detention, he made a right-hand turn onto Riverside Drive from a street a few blocks south of the apartment. I looked out for him at the estimated time he would be making the turn (until I learned to pick out Jack's car's headlights). I rushed to scoop up John into my arms. We hurried down the long hallway and out to the elevator so that John and I would be waiting when the elevator door opened to welcome Jack with a hug and a kiss.

Not long after we moved into the apartment we were told by one of our neighbors that an older couple on the first floor, whose apartment was directly below ours, had had a kitchen fire several years before. Later on I would remember those words.

It was early in the morning when we awakened to the sound of fire engines. Looking out of the window, we saw fire engines arriving on the street below. Flames could be seen starting to flicker out of a first-floor window directly below our kitchen window. We ran to get John and then ran down the hall to see if the stairs next to the elevators would provide a safe exit. The hall was already full of smoke, so the door was quickly closed. As we left the apartment, we saw smoke curling up between the three-inch-wide inlaid hardwood floors of the hall. We ran back to the fire escape window in the bedroom. Jack broke the window with my beloved RCA basketball trophy. Despite the urgency, I later felt very sad looking at my treasured trophy with the missing basketball at the end of the upraised arm.

As a fireman was very carefully helping baby John and myself down the fire truck's extended ladder, I was sobbing for my darling orange kitten that was still in the apartment. A *Daily News* photographer was snapping pictures. Three wonderful firemen went back into the apartment and rescued my cat. Before this cat, I had another cat, a darling little gray one. He had been impossible to save even with repeated veterinarian visits and a variety of medications, all of which we could ill afford. Both cats had come from animal shelters.

After the fire, the acrid smell of smoke in every room was so intense that the apartment had to be professionally cleaned. Despite the cleaning, headaches and the clinging smell of burning material persisted for weeks before finally fading and giving way to the woodsy smell of pine oil.

My cooking skills were rudimentary at best. Jack had invited a friend from Columbia University for dinner. I bought a chicken without knowing the difference between various labels. Everything might have turned out differently if I had boiled the chicken until it was tender and then added some dumplings to the broth. I cleaned and stuffed the bird with a nice stuffing straight out of the Betty Crocker cookbook that I have to this day. I knew to use a meat thermometer. In the meantime, the almost teetotaler Jack was sharing a bottle of whiskey with his friend. Thank God I opened the oven door. The meat thermometer I had placed in the chicken registered the right temperature, but the chicken didn't smell like what a finished roasted chicken should smell like. I started poking around the bird to discover the crop had been left in the bird. I hadn't noticed it when I was dressing the chicken for roasting. The crop is a pouch in the esophagus of the chicken that holds ingested chicken food with gastric juices for later digestion. After rinsing the bird and smearing butter on it, I served the chicken. I was ever so grateful they were feeling no pain and I got no complaints.

Our son, John, was an endless delight with his bounding energy, his infectious grin, and his laughter formed from deep within his little body. He easily socialized with other children. Jack and I delighted in his frequent escapades of one kind or another, but through all of this his words were few indeed. Could it be that the birth injury had somehow spared his advanced motor skills but damaged his ability to speak? We managed to get John accepted into a very small class of children at Columbia University, where both parents and the child were assessed and instructed. Parents' voices were taped and then sounded back to us to help us enunciate more clearly, speak more slowly, or do whatever might be helpful for our children's development. Other techniques included placing the child's hand on our throats so they could feel movement as we spoke, and putting their hands in front of our mouths as we spoke so they could get the feel for the in and out of air being part of producing sound. I don't know how much the class helped, but it wasn't long before John was a full-blown chatterbox. John was such a precious child, and I loved him so. The so-called terrible twos never came. He was a spunky, cheerful child.

On a cold, sunshine-filled winter day, a few inches of newly fallen snow gave a mantle of white to the banks of the Hudson River across the street from our apartment. I had John bundled in his usual winter clothes topped with a heavy red sweater and knit hat. I was helping him prepare to slide down a small sloping incline on his new little sled. A boy a few years older asked John if he could help him to go down the hill. John's instantaneous response was "If you think I need help, go to hell." What an unexpected statement! But I could not resist a little smile as I politely refused the boy's help.

We badly needed money, and I tried to find some kind of work. I managed to get a job as a telephone receptionist and worked, for a rather short time, when Jack was home with John. It was a company that fielded calls for theatrical people. One of the calls was for one of the Gabor sisters. When I called her, she seemed annoyed. I assumed she didn't think the call was important enough for her to be bothered. What did I know? Most of the calls were such that I could wing them, like an agent looking for a client booking or a client looking for an agent. The company kept me longer than the time period I was hired to cover.

*Daughter Theresa plays
under her father's cranked
upright pallet,
November 12, 1968.*

*Children of Jack and
Theresa, John Bryant and
Theresa Annette,
April 1960.*

*Children John and Theresa
with their mother, 1962.*

Chapter 4

Wanting a Second Child

The year was 1959. It wasn't too long before I started coaxing Jack for another kid. It wasn't that I dreamed of another boy or girl. I don't know why I felt some sense of urgency. I promised it would cost so little, I'd go through a clinic, etc. I think maybe it was partly to shut me up on the subject that he finally agreed to go ahead with the idea of a second child, despite our meager income. In addition, the baby was planned to come after December 1 and before January of the next year. After December 1, Jack's job insurance would cover the hospitalization at the Polyclinic Hospital and the doctor at the clinic. If the baby came before January 1 of the next year, we could get a few dollars of our income taxes as a deduction.

We sure had to get busy in a hurry, so sex was a daily activity. But one day we got home rather late. Jack looked at me. "I can't" came out of his mouth. I started to cry as we held each other and fell into a tearful sleep. It was about two in the morning when I got a gentle nudge. I'm sure that was the night I got pregnant with a beautiful little girl who we would call Theresa Annette.

I was twenty-nine years old and three and one-half months pregnant with our second child. I had managed to transform our Riverside Drive apartment into a cozy nest overlooking the Hudson River. On occasion our Spanish neighbors came to admire what I considered our quite lovely newly refurbished apartment. We were dreadfully poor, but there was such contentment.

During the time we lived in Manhattan, I worked on a number of sewing projects using paper patterns. After I got pregnant with the baby, I spent four months making a baptismal dress, hat, slip, and booties. All the seams were finished as French seams. Tiny pleats were at the shoulder of the dress as dainty pale-blue ribbon and lace trailed down the front. The embroidery was done with strands narrowed to one thread. Narrow strands of lace edged the dress's little puffy sleeves and neck, as well as the slip, the bonnet, and even the little booties. I made an orange-colored dress from a rather inexpensive material that I was never happy wearing. I made clothes for baby John by taking apart some of Jack's old clothes. They included a light-tan coat and matching hat, as well as both short and long pants. They looked store-bought, which made me quite proud.

I sewed a tailored suit for Jack. I had no idea how hard it was to get the material to form the underlying chest area in a man's suit, as well as make the collar lay just right. I worked so hard, hand stitching the edges of the collar, as well as down the front and on the pockets. There was only one thing that I couldn't seem to get just right. The lapels would not lay flat enough. Jack wore the jacket only a couple of times, though he did get good usage out of the pants part of the suit. My sewing skills using patterns actually got quite good, but there was the never-ending problem with not having enough money to buy material that would look, feel, and fall well.

During our several years in Manhattan, Jack seemed to be getting physically weaker. Jack finally went to Columbia University Hospital for a checkup. I was to find out years later that he had been diagnosed with possible amyotrophic lateral sclerosis (Lou Gehrig's disease). Jack withheld this information from me for many years.

Jack Santmann still able to sit upright shortly after starting the Little Flower Residence in Babylon, New York, 1962.

The four-apartment building in Babylon, New York, which was transformed into the Little Flower Residence as an adult home.

Chapter 5

We Had to Make a Change

We had to make a change. Jack got a job as a human factors engineer with Sperry Gyroscope Company at MacArthur Field in Ronkonkoma, New York.

We moved to Westbury, Long Island. There I managed to talk the school district into having the children each donate a can of food for the unemployed coal miners of West Virginia. They brought the cans to the school. I managed to get a women's group to bring the cans to my house. Getting a truck to ship the goods to Virginia was quite difficult, but finally I was able to send a truckload of food.

Jack's physical condition continued to deteriorate. He could no longer hold a pen. One incident had him trying to board the Long Island Railroad, falling, and being helped to his feet. The situation that ended his efforts at driving a car happened when he was coming off the Northern State Parkway to Brush Hollow Road. It was wintertime, and there was snow on the ground. His efforts to turn the steering wheel for the upcoming curve in the exit ramp were not sufficient. The front end of the car came to rest on top of a snow bank on the side of the ramp. It was then that the inevitable was obvious—his job was no longer an option, and he had to resign.

During the same time period, I began to think that there was something missing in my children's lives. Their only grandparents lived hundreds of miles from our Long Island home. I decided to try to find them grandparents by calling nursing homes to see if a patient residing in the nursing home might like to adopt a grandchild. I got out a phone book and called twelve nursing homes. With each call I was put off with annoyance. I decided to make one more call. The woman who answered the phone invited me to come over. I followed her directions.

As I arrived at the address, there rose before me what looked like a huge gray dilapidated mansion. The remains of what had been a garden entrance with a statuesque water fountain were run over with weeds. There was no running water. A wide metal strap circled one of the chimneys, as if holding it together. I knocked on the door. A man answered the door. I assumed he must be the butler. I told him I had been invited to come over. He led me inside and had me take a seat. The room was of magnificent proportions. One end held a massive stone fireplace. Five double French doors covered the far wall. A majestic curved staircase rose to the right. I looked around the room. Something was missing. There was no grandeur. There were many sofas, easy chairs, end tables adorned with ordinary lamps, and coffee tables arranged in various ways. The floor was covered with rubber tile. There were no signs of the room being used. There were no people in the room. In addition, there were no magazines, newspapers, ashtrays, knickknacks, or vases among the furnishings. Finally, the man who had let me in came back and led me to an enormous dining room with its own stone fireplace at the far end. There was a woman in the room who introduced herself and the man as Mr. and Mrs. Frank De Esposito. The man left the room as the woman and I sat down at a very long dining-room table. The conversation started with her telling me about her family. I told her about my family—the two children, the disabled husband, my searching for grandparents for my children because theirs either lived very far away or had already passed away. She changed the subject and started talking about the history of the mansion. There were forty-five rooms and seventeen bathrooms in the mansion, which was the fabled Jones Manor House. It had been completed in 1918 by Mary Elizabeth Jones. Then Mrs. De Esposito went on about the reason she had invited me to come and talk to her.

She and her husband had come into a small inheritance. They didn't want to go to a nursing institution. The mansion seemed like a good place to buy and transform into the Mimi Dee North Shore Rest Home. They would have twelve people live as residents to help defray the $40,000-per-year upkeep. Their dream hit a roadblock. They had applied to the local governing body for permission for twelve people to reside with them under rest home housing. They were denied. The maximum they would be allowed was nine. The expenses for the upkeep could not be carried by nine residents. She was looking for someone to take over the place.

Why Mrs. De Esposito invited me over based on the set of circumstances above, I had no idea. I knew nothing about adult homes. I was to learn that if a building was to be used to house elderly under an adult home license, first permission must be granted by the local Department of Social Services concerning the number of residents allowed, the location, the people asking for permission, etc. The ultimate authority rested with the Department of Social Services in Albany.

When I returned home, Jack and I reviewed the option of trying to open an adult home as a way to keep our family together. We had very little money. I called every Realtor in Nassau County, trying to rent a building with the concept of opening an adult home. As soon as my situation was described, the conversation came to an abrupt end. Finally, I came up with the idea of putting a personal ad in *Newsday*, stating that I was looking for a building to rent to start an adult home. I got a call from a woman who owned several adult homes in Lindenhurst, Long Island. She owned a four-apartment building in Babylon, Long Island, that might be converted to an adult home. It was a building that had been built as a summer home by a man with twelve children in 1900. The family name was Lawrence. Many years later, the house had been sold and converted into four apartments.

The year was 1962, and we struck a deal. We would pay rent every month for five years, and at the end of five years there would be a balloon payment due of $38,000. By the time we moved to Babylon, Jack was an unemployed quadriplegic, and we were living on Jack's Social Security and Veterans Disability benefits.

I got permission to open an adult home in the Babylon apartment building. A critical part of getting some money together to be able to continue was that the company that Jack had worked for finally paid off on two $10,000 life insurance policies before his death, based on two doctors' assurances that he was terminally ill with a short life expectancy.

During the years from the late fifties to when Jack died in 1976, my primary goals were trying to get him cured, keeping the family together, and trying to make our family life as normal as possible. For years there were mostly fourteen- to eighteen-hour workdays consisting of spackling, painting, cooking, cleaning, plumbing, bookkeeping, and directing employees, all while trying to be a good wife and mother. At first, most of the employees were mental patients on a work-release program who lived on the premises. I had converted the third floor into living quarters.

I renovated the four-apartment building one room at a time into an adult home. The necessary living-room furniture came from as far back as my single days before I married Jack. A commercial three-well sink, stove, tray racks, trays, and dishes came from a restaurant supply store for the kitchen. The first bedroom furniture came from Sears Roebuck. I bought the dining-room tables, chairs, and bed linens from a Korvette's store. I bargained at every turn, trying to get everything for less money than the marked prices.

For a number of years after the Babylon apartment house became our home, I moved the family from one unfinished room to the next in order to prepare our most recently occupied room with spackling, painting, and furnishing so that we could admit another resident into the ever-expanding Little Flower Residence. When the main building became fully occupied, we built an addition of several floors between a small cottage on the property and the four-apartment main building.

Jack moved into a room at the end of a hall that was being used as an office. A very special employee, a lovely person named Ann Dini, was giving him very good care. She fed him, bathed him, and was at his beck and call. She also provided a special place in my toddler Theresa's life, taking her to the park to play on the playground and to feed the ducks.

After all the bedrooms had been renovated and adult home residents added, there were no bedrooms available for my children and myself, so we were forced to move to the third floor with the employees from the hospital. The room was very small. There were bunk beds for the children against one wall. On the opposite wall under the slant of the roof and only three feet away from the bunk beds was my single bed. Because of the noise of the other occupants of the third floor and my own easily awakened status, there was a rather desperate measure that I tried.

It was late in the evening. I left John junior in our tiny third-floor sleeping quarters and loaded two-year-old Theresa in the back of our black Plymouth car to go looking for a quiet street. I found a northwest section of the village with no people on the street. I managed to go to sleep. I didn't know how long I had been sleeping when there was a knock on the car window. A man standing there wanted to know if I was okay. When I briefly described to him what I was doing, he quietly said, "Come here any time." I have no words to describe my embarrassment. Another time on the same quest, I went to the Babylon Railroad station in the quiet of night to try to get some rest. It was not to be. I hadn't been there for very long before I realized this was not a good place to be found by just anybody while parked in a darkened car at the railroad station. I went back to the third floor.

Over many years, Jack was given different treatments to make him well. Jack found out about a doctor in Florida who furnished snake venom for trials in medical research. He got an address, and I flew to Florida in search of the venom. The visit was a rather strange one. I rented a car and followed the directions I had been given. I went through what looked like a comfortable middle-class community of homes with waterways wending their way here and there, covered by small bridges leading from one section to another. Finally, the building with the address I was looking for came into view. It sure didn't look like a clinic or medical facility of any kind. I was ushered inside and asked a few questions, and then I was given the venom. I was made to understand that the doctor expected to get some money, but having none, I quickly exited. I brought the venom home, and then it was up to Jack and the doctor to figure out how to introduce the venom into his system.

During our years at 146 North Carll Avenue in Babylon, New York, there were many trips to Monmouth Medical Center in Long Branch, New Jersey. First a little handmade elevator was put into a cut-out piece of the wooden porch floor of the house. A van was outfitted in the back with a lift that could be lowered to ground level and electrically lifted to the height of the vehicle floor for entrance. Then the doors would be closed, and the lift was brought flush with the rear of the vehicle. The lift mechanism was a source of never-ending problems, from glitches of the lift not lifting or lowering, to getting stuck at various levels, especially in bitter cold weather.

One especially memorable trip was on the icy Belt Parkway to the Verrazano-Narrows Bridge. When I reached the bridge, which had its share of ice and snow, the van was especially hard to manage. The wheels were not griping. I kept the van creeping up the rather sharp curve of the entrance ramp, trying to move at a pace that would keep us from stopping or sliding sideways in either direction. At a snail's pace I managed to get to the level plane of the bridge itself.

Chapter 6

Wicky One, 1963

The year was 1963. A second extension had been built between the Little Flower Residence and a second three-story building called the Little Flower Residence Annex. My husband, Jack, was housed in the second extension. My two children, our two Siamese cats, and I were in the third floor of the annex. The first two floors provided living quarters for residents of the Little Flower Annex. The third floor access was obtained by climbing two flights of the fire escape.

Jack had mentioned on several occasions how nice it would be to have a boat. I had been raised nowhere near a large body of water, so I wasn't of a mind-set to encourage that endeavor. Employees would hold the phone for him, allowing him to research the possibilities of boat ownership. He managed to locate a thirty-seven-foot Norwalk boat and have it shipped from one of the New England states to a marina in Nassau County. It was called *Wicky One*. He then somehow got it outfitted with a boom that was shipped from someplace in Florida.

The boom was mounted on the deck with an extended arm that allowed it to swing from its mounting to my convertible dockside, as well as the deck itself and the fly bridge. There was an electric component to the boom that allowed a pulley contraption to swing over to my car, lift Jack out of the car, swing him over to the deck of the boat, and lower him into a specially constructed chair with the appropriate hardware and wiring on the deck of the boat. Four metal plates at each setting in the flooring of the deck, the main salon, and the fly bridge allowed Jack to be securely fastened at any of the three locations.

At our home in Babylon, I used a Hoyer Lift with its cloth seat attached to metal rings to place him in my convertible. The seat of the Hoyer Lift was left under him as I drove the car to *Wicky One's* number-nine docking spot at the Babylon Village main dock on the Great South Bay.

I hadn't yet developed the skills needed to run a boat. At the time I wasn't even sure whether I would like running a boat, the Great South Bay, the ocean, different waterways, etc. It didn't matter. Jack planned a trip and hired a captain. *Wicky One* was going to take us out to the Fire Island Inlet and south along the coast past New York City and along the New Jersey coastline to a Pennsylvania Inlet.

We planned the trip weeks ahead of time. I was uneasy. In the few outings with *Wicky*, we seemed to run out of gas rather quickly. There were two gauges indicating the amount of gas in each of the two tanks supplying each of the two motors. Whenever the boat had been run for a rather abbreviated time frame, one tank would read nearly empty while the second tank would read nearly full.

At last the big day came. Small craft warnings had been posted. The hired captain was uneasy. How could a trip, weeks in the planning, be postponed? Jack was determined to make the trip, and I was too much of a neophyte to adamantly refuse to put all of our lives in danger. Jack had acted as the leader and supervisor in our family in almost every way imaginable from the very onset of his quadriplegic condition. Off we went.

The trip to the Fire Island Inlet was rather uneventful. Jack insisted on being on the flying bridge with the captain. Our children, John and Theresa, were down below with me. It didn't take long to realize the dreadful situation we had gotten ourselves into. Waves washed over the hull and tossed us about. Everyone was getting seasick except me. Water was coming into the boat around the windows. I had chewing gum and told the kids to chew and give me the gum as I tried, with a feeble effort, to keep water from pouring into the bilge in one way or another. Later I realized scuppers hadn't been put into the fish line opening on the sides of the boat, letting in untold amounts of seawater. I had no way of knowing whether a bilge pump might be working or even if we had one.

Someone told me that I needed to go to the flying bridge to fasten Jack's head down, as it was being thrown from side to side. I took a white cotton sheet with me. It's a wonder that neophytes ever live through the trials and tribulations of life. I wasn't wearing a life jacket as I struggled to hold on to and climb the short ladder to the flying bridge. The mountainous waves continued to thrash the boat around in great, angry upheaval. Sunglasses in my pocket got crushed against the ladder. Finally reaching Jack, I got his head tied down and returned to the cabin. Of course, by the time we were well into the ocean, it seemed as if the choices were equal in danger. How could going on in this angry sea be any worse than turning around with the threat of broadsiding waves, as well as facing the Fire Island Inlet with its tricky shoals and narrow passageway, which were challenging in the best of weather?

The hours seemed endless as we proceeded west off the Long Island coast to New York Harbor and then south along the Jersey coast. Finally, a navigable inlet presented itself. As we turned west into the inlet, the high winds and lashing rain were still a threat. Our ultimate goal was finding a marina that could accommodate us. We were no more than several hundred yards inside the inlet when the boat's motors sputtered and became silent.

I had warned the captain of a possible problem, as one gas gauge had always registered in the full position even when we were putting gas in the boat, which seemed to indicate we were only filling the amount that was what one tank would hold. He didn't believe me. He kept trying to make the motors respond as he kept pushing the start buttons. After a very short time of the motors giving only tiny sputters of life, he finally gave up the effort. We made a marine radio call for help. An anchor was thrown overboard to keep us from drifting. The storm had abated to only a lesser degree. Visibility was still very limited with the wind and rain lashing at us.

Finally, off in the distance appeared a man who can only be described as heaven-sent. He was dressed in a yellow slicker and hood, and he was coming toward us in a small skiff. He was fighting rough waters and thrashing rain. Finally, there he was next to our boat. He had a rather large container of gas. The effort seemed endless, but finally some gas made it into the gas tank. We continued to be blessed. A marina was located fairly close by, and a dock was available.

The stubborn captain tried to start the motors but had burned out one of the motor's starters. By some incredible blessing, personnel at the marina where we were finally moored were able to find a new one in the vicinity.

Later, after mechanic after mechanic tried to address *Wicky's* problem, it was finally discovered. A hose feeding gas to the motors was resting on the bottom of a gas tank.

There was to be no captain other than myself from that day on. I learned to not only love the boat but I got quite good at manipulating the effects from the wind and currents, addressing water depths and navigable waterways, and handling the boat under different conditions. There were many adventures that followed, some more memorable than others. Jack loved the boat and was not reluctant to ask me to undertake rather difficult assignments.

The most challenging navigational feat I ever accomplished was piloting the *Wicky* with my disabled husband, two young children, and one aide for Jack on our thirty-seven-foot boat on a two-week trip from the waterways of Babylon, New York, to Canada.

I left Babylon and crossed the Great South Bay to the Fire Island Inlet and then turned west in the Atlantic Ocean toward New York City. I turned north up the Hudson River and through the locks that I had never navigated or witnessed. Finally, there was Lake Champlain. I attained my ultimate goal of pulling up to a dock in Canada and disembarking for a few minutes before turning and triumphantly heading home.

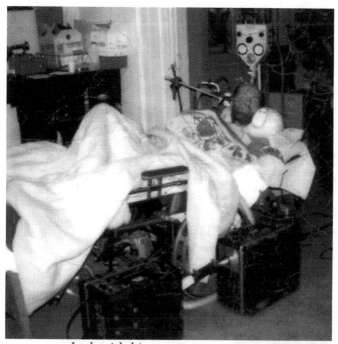

*Jack with his many
means of life support, 1972.*

*Theresa as the
proprietress of the Little
Flower Residence.*

Chapter 7

Building Little Flower Nursing Home

There was a mounting pile of freshly dug earth at the 1972 construction site of what was to be the Little Flower Nursing Home in East Islip, New York. The smaller digs were for precast cesspools.

My husband, John, a quadriplegic with amyotrophic lateral sclerosis, was a patient at Good Samaritan Hospital in their intensive care unit, and he was struggling to stay alive.

I returned a call from James Canellos, the architect on the job. He said that more cesspools were needed because the previous test for the height of the water table was not accurate. It was twelve feet, not sixteen feet.

John and I had always made all business decisions together. When I told Jim I was in the hospital with what might be a dying husband and that I would get back to him, his response was quick and sharp. "If you don't give me the authority to do what is needed on the job, I'm quitting."

John was a particularly tightfisted skeptic of all matters concerning spending. After all, extras on the job meant a percent of the cost of extras went to the architect. Money was very tight. My name was the only one listed as "owner" on all the paperwork for the Little Flower Nursing Home, so the final decision had to be mine.

I was the administrator of the Little Flower Residence in Babylon, New York. We had two children, eleven-year-old Theresa Annette and fourteen-year-old John Bryant.

It was as if someone had their hands on my throat and was squeezing out the last hope of ever getting the nursing home built. I realized if he left the job, I could not resurrect further effort by myself and with John. There had been such a struggle to get to where we were on this project. After what seemed like an eternity, I came to realize I had absolutely no choice. I gave Jim the authority to continue the job, using his discretion on extras. When John and I first had the idea of building a nursing home where he might be better cared for than our house across the street from the Little Flower Residence, there were many challenges. At the time, his needs were being addressed by an intercom system jury-rigged from the residence to a mic next to him. If an employee heard him calling at any time of the day or night, he or she was to come across the street to address his needs. It was a system that was filled with trial-and-error mistakes of every magnitude, from both equipment and employee response.

Building a nursing home necessitated addressing a multitude of challenges. Research was done to find the proper sequence of mandatory events in the long and arduous process. The first challenge was to find a need for nursing home beds in Suffolk County in the proximity of our home in Babylon, as determined by the New York State Health Department. I needed to find land zoned to meet local building requirements to build a nursing home with enough acreage to accommodate what we were hoping would be a successful business venture of 160 nursing home beds. At the same time I was finding out about the entire New York State process under what is called New York State's Certificate of Need. It was daunting and never-ending filing appropriate paperwork, appearing before state and local boards, architectural plans that needed to meet exact specifications for every space.

Innovation was needed to find any land that might meet the basic requirements to build our dreamed-of nursing home. The sophistication of the real estate market was primitive compared to the market today. I drove the streets of the south shore, looking for land that might be a desirable location, have the right business zoning, and be large enough to accommodate our plans. An empty lot on Montauk Highway in East Islip next to a shopping center seemed perfect.

Inquiries revealed an owner in Connecticut had future plans to extend the shopping center into the empty lot. There was a local real estate agent named Pat Kramer involved with another deal with the owner, so he became my agent. He had thinning slicked-back hair. He wore tight-fitting polyester suits over a slightly rotund stomach, and the requisite boots over which hung the boot-bottom trousers. He was a fast-talking city slicker who assumed a very superior air. In trying to get the owner to accept an offer to buy the land, he turned out to be the kind of salesman the job needed. The deal was very close to being made, but I wasn't getting calls returned from the agent. Finally, I found out he was in jail. I needed him. I called the jail and found out he would be released if a cash bail of five thousand dollars was paid. I got a promise of a return of the bail money from Kramer, paid the bail, and got him out of jail.

For me, the most memorable and first meeting of the entire building of Little Flower Nursing Home happened in our small home across the street from the Little Flower Residence. John was in his usual place a few feet from the front door. He was strapped in a slightly elevated position to an engineered six-and-a-half-foot padded wooden pallet that allowed him to be cranked from being flat on his back to an almost upright position. A bird respirator was nearby, with a plastic tube feeding oxygen directly to a mouthpiece for Jack to draw on its supply at any moment. His body was obviously wasted. A card table had been set up in the room with chairs around it. The men coming to the meeting were a lawyer; Bob Nova, a builder; and Jim Canellos, an architect.

Horrified looks greeted us at the door. The men, obviously in a great deal of discomfort, sat down. The conversation was mostly with them and Jack. At first it was as if they were humoring us, but it wasn't long before the conversation actually turned heated as terms and conditions of possible contracts were tossed back and forth.

There would be many more seemingly insurmountable obstacles to overcome before we accepted the first patient in October 1973.

Years later I was told I was the first woman in the state of New York to get an FHA loan for a nursing home with only a woman's name on the application and subsequent approval.

Theresa with her two children, John and Theresa,
on a QE 2 Atlantic voyage with a friend of John's, 1969.

John Jr. and Theresa
Annette posing.

Theresa Annette
ready for her favorite pastime,
riding horses.

Chapter 8

Solo Cross-Country

During my first flying lesson and due to my instructor's miscalculations, I had already experienced a storm that closed in before we got back to our home base at Zahn's Airport. We were in a very old plane, made of what looked like a yellow fabric tightly woven over a visibly skeletal frame. The dual controls were a stick between the legs and pedals for the feet of the student and the flight instructor. We soon were in the middle of the storm. Rain was pelting the windshield, making visibility a matter of a few feet. Lighting and thunder added to the frenetic environment. Even though the controls indicated that we were at two hundred feet, the ground was not visible. The turbulence was so violent that I had to hang on to the seat to keep from hitting the overhead material. Finally, my instructor said that we were over Republic Airport. "Please take it down," I begged. He didn't answer. I think he was too embarrassed to land at another airport that was just across a graveyard and Route 109 from our intended Zahn destination. I was terrified as we bounced in our tiny box of a rattling plane over the barely visible graveyard and then over 109 to Zahn's very short runways.

There was another time that my instructor wanted to practice his wing-over-wing rolls in a Cessna 160, in which I was getting a flying lesson. He already had the impression that I wouldn't talk to someone negatively or complain about him. I never did. After eight rolls, when my stomach was turning along with the plane (and I'm sure I was green), the pilot took a five-minute break and then did four more rolls before starting my lesson. It's a good thing I trusted him, although in retrospect I'm not sure why I did.

It was to be my first and only solo cross-country, a mandatory requirement before taking the test for a pilot's license. The day began with my arriving at Zahn's Airport a little later than I should have. My favorite Cessna 160 was already in the air, so I had to settle for the only one available. The usual procedures were completed: filing a flight plan (the route from Zahn's to the Flying H Airport in New Jersey), landing, gassing the plane, performing all the plane checks, taking off, flying to Atlantic City, gassing the plane, performing the plane checks, and flying back to Zahn's. The flight plan included approximate arrival times at the different destinations, compass headings, taking into account winds, etc. Then there was the lengthy and tiresome preboarding checklist—check that gas tanks are full, move the ailerons back and forth, after boarding check the instruments, rev the engine to the appropriate rpm, etc. One time I forgot to check the altimeter. On the final approach when coming in for a landing, I wondered why I was so close to the ground. The altimeter was off by over one hundred feet. I had forgotten to set it before the flight. I realized my error after I landed.

Finally, it was time to get permission from ground control for takeoff. Even though takeoff is the most dangerous aspect of flying, for me it never seemed to be threatening unless I was on that grotesquely short east–west runway at Zahn's. To add to the colorful east–west runway aura of danger, there was a rather low pole wiring close to the end of the runway and a graveyard across the highway. That morning I took the much longer north–south runway. Running at full throttle and heading into the wind, I was airborne after using only one-half to two-thirds of the runway.

Following the compass heading, I was first over the ocean. Then I reached land, which, according to my mental calculations, must be New Jersey. Then I ran into a bit of a problem. There was just enough snow on the ground to make some of the map's landmarks such as a drive-in theater, to be of much less value. Juggling the maps, using the controls to keep the plane at the right height and level, and trying to correlate the Omni station on the map with the Omni indicator on the plane's instrument panel were all very frustrating and scary tasks. Would I ever find the Flying H? I was so proud when, even sooner than I expected, I found the airport. I landed, gassed up, went through the entire checklist, got airborne, and repeated the same procedure in Atlantic City, though in Atlantic City the proximity of water to the runway was a bit unnerving.

Now I was home free. All I had to do was visually follow the Jersey coast and then fly over New York Harbor to Coney Island and Jones Beach and then to Zahn's Airport. There were three land visualizations by car, by boat, and by plane that presented very differently around the Manhattan area and I assumed in other areas, as well. This led to suppositions of land configurations that may not be realistic if the appropriate maps and charts were not being utilized. As I was leaving Atlantic City, the journey along the Jersey coast heading north was rather relaxing and certainly enjoyable. I was holding at two thousand feet. My Cessna 160 was purring. I felt confident with visual navigation. Time went on, and the Manhattan skyline was not coming into view. I still felt optimistic until rather suddenly I realized that streetlights were going on below me. I certainly had never done any flying at night, so I started getting very anxious. Next I figured that if I pushed every switch that I could see to the *on* position, probably most of my plane's lights would go on. If there was another small plane in the air around me without the benefit of radar, then I could be seen. Also I would be visible to the Kennedy Airport air traffic controllers so they could divert the big planes around me, as my flight path took me very close to the airport.

Finally, I saw Coney Island off in the distance. I needed to make a right-hand turn and keep the island on my left. By now darkness was closing in. The runway lights of the airport were coming up on my left. They looked mighty inviting, but my resolve held. Visualization indicated a jutting of a thin strip of land parallel to the mainland, with a bridge connecting it to the mainland and the large airport with its many runways. Presumably Kennedy was northwest of the bridge. I was right on course. A moment or two later, sheer terror placed a tight grip around my throat. I felt as if I could not possibly get enough oxygen. I was again seeing the same set of landmarks; a large airport with its multiple runways was northwest of a jutting thin strip of land parallel to the mainland, with a bridge connecting it to the mainland. How could I possibly have made a 360-degree turn over the beach without knowing it? A quick flash of this happening to people lost in the woods or lost in a storm went through my mind. There were other urgent flashes. *Land on the beach, bring this damn plane down, and use the end of one of the long runways. I must not. Get it together, for God's sake.*

Look at your compass, and believe it. It was on an east heading. I made myself use it as my definitive point of reference all the way to the glorious lights of the Zahn runway. I called ahead for landing instructions, which to me had always sounded as undecipherable as the hieroglyphics on London's Cleopatra's Needle. On this day they were no more understood than before. It didn't matter anyway. Neither did the direction of the wind sock. I was coming in using the closest end of the runway, whether the wind was with me or against me.

There were several people who had panicked at my nighttime arrival, including one of the owners of the airport, who was awaiting my arrival and had left the runway lights on for me. My husband, John, had been frantically calling the airport, trying to find out where I was. I bounced a few times coming in, because I pulled back a little too soon, which initiated a stall. I wouldn't have cared if I had bounced the entire length of the runway.

The confusion of the two airports was that there was an airport that laypeople were not familiar with. It was called Floyd Bennett Field, which was located across a bridge and north of Far Rockaway. John F. Kennedy Airport was a few miles northeast of Floyd Bennett Field and has a bridge connecting it to the easternmost portion of the island of Far Rockaway. Being alone as a novice pilot with no nighttime experience, even in retrospect, seemed pretty scary.

Chapter 9

A Son Leaves Home

It was twelve o'clock at night on October 1, 1973. A few lights across the river were throwing their dancing reflections in jagged lines over the water. The air was hot, muggy, and as still as death. The grasshoppers were carrying on their endless chirping. Every slowly exhaled breath hung motionless in the still air. The cat was going about his usual rounds of food, litter box, and cleaning himself on the bed. I felt so devastated. A part of me was being torn away. I had struggled to make my son independent, even though there was such a great need within me to keep him close to me always. I could not, would not, hold him. Oh, how I wished that dependence was what was best for him. No matter how I twisted and turned, I must make him free. Up to this point I had been so sophisticated. My attitudes and actions were based on what I considered best for him. I had repressed my feelings about our parting until the final moment. All human encounters that are truly worthwhile seem to end in such painful parting.

For years I had directed, prodded, loved, and manipulated, and now for the first and last time, the flight from the nest was complete. Never again would there be the nightly ritual of my knowing when he was in his bed. In the past, no matter how late he came in, I knew that he was finally secure in the comfort of a familiar and caring environment.

From now on he must face the world as best he could. What face would it present to him? Would it be kind and gentle or brutal and harsh? Would Johns Hopkins be caring or indifferent as it challenged and stimulated him? How I wished that these days, which seemed endless until now, would last a little longer. I felt as if I had been leading up to his leaving forever, and yet I was not prepared at all. I could not believe the time had finally arrived.

Oh God, why do you torment me so? Do you give only to take? Every time I seem to find some peace of mind, you somehow find some way to rip it from me. Maybe I'm blaming you too much. I don't know what you really have in mind. Do you want me to love more or less or not at all, or don't you care?

Tomorrow, five hours from now, John would leave for college. From that moment on, my influence would no longer be paramount. Professors, girls, and business acquaintances would be the major moving forces shaping his life.

John, you are such a vacillating mixture of man and child. You are constantly changing. One moment you are a demanding, assertive, arrogant know-it-all, and the next moment you are a questioning, searching, insecure boy in need of moral support. I know I tended to spoil the boy with things like a motorboat at fourteen and a car at seventeen, but I also made demands of the man, such as self-discipline and high grades in school. Were my motives pure? I called none self-serving, but were they? Or was I looking for reflected glory?

Should I have asked for more or less? I really don't think so, unless I should have been more forceful about having John pick up after himself. All I had to go on was how I felt about what I saw as he left with such sadness in his eyes.

From the time he was an infant, I was told by the prophets of doom, "Wait until the terrible twos. Wait until he starts school. Wait until he's a teenager. Wait until he goes to college." I had waited, and they were truly wrong. I continued to enjoy John from the first time I held him in my arms.

On John's first birthday, I gave him a party at our Philadelphia house. He went running from one end of the house to the other, making delightful laughing sounds. As the years passed John was very early to walk and run, while his talking was a slower process. Many years later with testing and tutors in Babylon New York's high school he was the top math and science student. So many memories of John came and went, which only heightened the desire to keep him with me. There were brief hours when I had been very angry with John, but sooner or later he or I always managed to concede and say, "I'm sorry." We once had such a violent quarrel, and that I told him to leave. He left as if he would never return, only to come back a few hours later. We agonized so over reconciliation.

I shall always love John for the single red rose, for the tender concern over parental quarrels, for his wanting me to be friends with his peers, for his getting terribly upset when his father was so sick, for his saying so if he thought I looked particularly nice, for giving me a dance when I was chaperoning, for buying a dumb-looking clown for my birthday, and for being so proud of his sister.

John sometimes said ugly things. Sometimes he said loving things. Which did he mean? Did it matter? Could I find in other endeavors the same satisfaction that I found in talking to him for hours on end, sometimes until two or three in the morning? Was there any other satisfaction as great as seeing a rambunctious roughneck turning into a responsible, mature adult? Did I do John justice? Would I be as proud of him in the future as I was today? I didn't want to feel this strongly about John's leaving. I was doing so well up to this evening. I had even talked myself into believing that I would be happy not to see the wet towel from the pool on the kitchen table, the scuba gear on the bench, and the ice chest on the kitchen floor. As annoyed as they all made me, dear God, what a small price to pay for a part of his being here at home with me. It was five thirty, and he was gone. I felt moments of anger toward him for leaving, as I felt anger directed toward me for encouraging him to leave one year early. Did I do right by him? Quiet gently surrounded and enveloped me. The dog was lying on the floor by the bed, and the cat had just left the room. The horizon outside was taking on a distinct dark-blue form as the houses across the river were slowly taking shape. The birds were now adding their early-morning sounds to the chirping grasshoppers. A misty haze was floating lazily a few feet over the water, with wisps of it drifting over the lawn. I felt empty and exhausted. Tears came no more. I would sleep.

John Sr. and Jr., with wife
and mother, Theresa, 1971.

Chapter 10

Jack Santmann Hospitalization

Jack had not been feeling well for several months. The complaints had started shortly after the chest respirator was initiated simultaneously with the bird respirator. First it was a general malaise, then a virus infection, and then an elevating temperature. When I arrived in the morning, the usual greeting became "I don't feel well." It was so easy to overlook a gradually deteriorating situation. There had been no dramatic gasping for breath until finally the fateful day arrived.

I had been out for the afternoon of April 19, 1971. I got home at about nine o'clock in the evening. At approximately eleven o'clock I was called by Dr. Pettit from Good Samaritan Hospital. Jack was in the emergency room in critical condition and insisting I not be called. As always, he tried to shield me from his medical condition as best he could while maintaining his self-imposed macho independence. My brother Pete had been living with us for a period of time. He was at the hospital, and under Jack's command he would not call me. Dr. Pettit overrode Jack's objections and called me. Dr. Schick had been called as a consult.

By the time I arrived at the hospital, Jack was struggling for every breath. Panic was evident on his white, drawn face. The doctors were desperately trying to determine a way to aerate him while he was being transferred from his wheelchair to a stretcher to take him to the operating room for an arterial cut down and possibly a tracheostomy. The feelings that battled for control of me were many. When I first saw him, the awful realization of the gravity of the situation struck me with a terrible force. I had rationalized away this last illness as I had many times before. It was tolerable to live with current problems from day to day. It was not tolerable to live with death from day to day on a long-term basis if the person in question was dear to you. Now there was no choice, but even so I could not face the idea of his almost immediate death. We were in the emergency room, and I had bitterly cried over signing papers for a tracheostomy. I had been told by Dr. Asa that if a tracheostomy was ever performed on Jack, he would not survive.

There were hurried conferences, rushing doctors and nurses, and then the blow. I leaned down to try to give Jack some comfort. As my head neared his, the horrible, unmistakable, sickly sweet smell of death jarred me to the core. He was going to die. I had smelled that same odor quite a few times just before someone died in our Little Flower Residence. It had always meant death—and usually very soon. It was as if I had been dealt a heavy blow to my midsection. Breath came in short pants. We had been through so damn much together, and here was the inevitable. The threat that had been hanging over my head all these years was here. It was really here. I moved away. Bitter tears stung my eyes. We had been through so much. The rest home had been one long, almost impossible struggle. We had fought the terrible handicaps under which we had started the business, with no money and no expertise. We fought the world. We fought each other.

After years in which we desperately struggled to survive, we had finally seen a rainbow on our horizon. We had gotten permission to build a nursing home and health-related facility. The fight to get it built had seemed to never end. First it was to be a lease back; that route was abandoned, and an FHA-backed loan finally had been attained. The struggle had taken not only a great deal of perseverance but also manipulating, knowledgeable people in many fields, such as real estate, law, and FHA, while learning what was going on. Jack had worked for four years, making endless phone calls and arranging meetings. The ground had been broken for what was to be the Little

Flower Nursing Home and Health-Related Facility about two weeks before that awful day on April 19.

I thoroughly disliked the dealings involved with starting a business. I had looked to Jack for maintaining a protective shield between me and the rough-and-tumble of business. Now the shield was being stripped away. I knew nothing of past negotiations or how to maintain the current ones. This quadriplegic who needed assistance for the very air he breathed was leaving me in a helpless embryonic state. Damn it, where was God? I knew I liked him and, up till now, thought we had a pretty good working relationship.

I said to Jack, "I'm taking your respirator away while you are being transferred to a stretcher." His immediate hostile response was "Like hell you are." Instant hate welled in his eyes. I drew back. What a quandary. He had always given orders with such assurance, and here he was desperately threatening me to dare take away his lifeline.

After what seemed like hours but must have been minutes, the doctors decided that he would be wheeled to the operating room floor in his own wheelchair, and there he would be intubated. I was allowed to get gowned and to go with Jack and the doctors past the swinging doors leading to the operating rooms. There in the corridor the intubation procedure was started. I was familiar enough with the procedure to not feel a great deal of apprehension about the procedure itself, but what followed left me even more apprehensive and miserable than I had been.

The doctor that was to do the procedure was an old pro and moved with a great deal of assurance. The anesthetist started removing Jack's mouthpiece from the bird and was trying to introduce a mask. Jack was fighting desperately but at last lost strength and became flaccid. The long large dark-red tube that was to be introduced down his throat seemed huge. It was about eighteen inches long and three-quarters of an inch in diameter. The end was not tapered, and as the doctor started to introduce it down Jack's throat there seemed to be an obstruction partway down his throat. The tube was rammed down again and again with no success. Jack's color was beginning to change to a reddish blue. At this point the doctor's controlled and measured movements had changed to very hurried and tense ones. The rubber tube was beginning to come back from the thrust with blood on the introducing end. A long metal rod with a pear-shaped end was put down the center of the rubber tube, and this was then rammed down his throat. After about three more futile attempts, it finally slipped down past the obstruction. For the last several tries I couldn't look anymore. Tears were falling and my throat was being squeezed along with my stomach. I was gently told that Jack was all right now that his airway had been secured. What an awful thing to have sticking out of his mouth, but that first sight was mild compared to sights that were to come.

Jack was wheeled down the hall to an operating room on the right. I was told, "No, you cannot go into the operating room." I went back through the swinging doors where both Dr. Pettit and Dr. Schick had been waiting in case they were needed. I had never met the kind of touching concern that I experienced during this hospital horror. Dr. Schick went to great lengths to tenderly advise me of what had been and what was probably going to be happening in a realistic but always hopeful manner. I shall always love him.

I finally went back through the swinging doors and down the hall to peer through the small window of the door to the operating room where Jack was being given both an arterial and a venous cut down. I had never seen one being done before and was completely unprepared for the sight that greeted me. His terribly thin arm had been strapped to the table, and an artery had been cut for the introduction of a very thin piece of plastic tubing so that blood could be frequently drawn to test for carbon dioxide and other irregularities. His wrist and hand were bathed in bright-red blood, and the floor was splattered with what looked like pools of blood. What god-awful additional trauma was his poor emaciated body being subjected to?

Jack was finally wheeled down to the intensive care unit. There he was placed in the glass-walled cage directly in front of the glass-walled nursing station. I pleaded with Dr. Schick to please let me, a registered nurse, stay by Jack's side. Everyone, including the charge RN, the inhalation therapist, and Dr. Schick, was very reluctant to have me stay, but Dr. Schick persevered. I was allowed to stay as many hours as I could stand.

When Jack came back from the OR to intensive care, an ammo bag was used for aeration. That awful tube was protruding from his mouth. It was connected to a Bennett MA-1 ventilator so his air could be carefully monitored. A large plug of rolled adhesive tape had been placed next to the tube in his mouth to keep him from unknowingly biting down on his own airway.

I think that I shall never pass the edifice that is Good Samaritan Hospital without mixed feelings of thanksgiving, uneasiness, and relief. How many others' vigils have ended with the ultimate futile grief of death? The days stretched out, with critical situations virtually touching. One would abate slightly only to have another plunge Jack again into barely living from hour to hour.

From his left arm the arterial line was connected to a machine with a small pump that served to maintain a slight pressure against the constantly moving saline solution into his body. The arterial blood was kept from coming into the tube, where it would clot. Into his left arm various solutions were introduced through a venous line. In addition, a catheter had been placed in his penis to prevent him from soiling himself. As I stood next to Jack's bed, his white, still form lay very still for a long time. Even in his drugged sleep, his face looked tense and anxious. With the first movement of his eyes, his mouth started to move, with his tongue making slow pushing motions against the plug of rolled tape that was the obstruction in his mouth. No sound could come out. His eyes gradually came into focus. Their reflected inner torment was so great that even a year and a half later the very thought of them made tears pour down my face. Jack, since becoming totally disabled, had ruled his world with his voice. Now every last vestige of control was lost. Every word, every movement, everything, the very air he breathed and the amounts he could breathe, were being dictated to him. The agony that pooled in those eyes tore at me with a cruel and brutal hand.

I tried. Oh, how I tried. One blink meant no; two blinks meant yes. Did he understand two blinks? He tired fast. Several questions, such as "Do you want to be moved?" and "Are you hungry" were all that he seemed capable of concentrating on before he would drift off again into a semicomatose state. Arterial blood was being taken every couple of hours to see if the carbon dioxide level was going up. The petcock was turned to feed the red blood down the line where it would be put in a test tube and placed on ice and then rushed to the lab. It seemed to me that to most of the staff this entire procedure was a hopeless effort, but Dr. Schick persevered through the most hopeless situations that were laced with my frequent bitter despair.

One of the most difficult decisions for a physician to make must be to go completely against a relative's pleading, sobbing rejoinder. It seemed to me his knowledge would probably lead him to delicately weigh what may be physically and/or psychologically deleterious to an already terribly overburdened patient. Did relatives give off bad vibes that were detrimental to the patient's well-being if the doctor didn't heed their words?

Dr. Schick hadn't used the tracheotomy procedure on that first night. My tearful reminders of sure death if it was used may have influenced him somewhat. No matter. I was so sure I was right. Dr. Asa had thoroughly brainwashed me. It would kill Jack—if not when it was being put in, then surely not long after the insertion.

My hours in the hospital started at seven in the morning and ended at eleven or later at night. I spent endless hours the first couple of days trying to understand what Jack wanted and trying to make him comfortable. No matter what I did, somehow I knew, it was not what he was trying to make me understand. His frustration was no less than mine. For endless sessions he looked and I asked, but I could never understand what those haunted eyes were trying so hard to tell me.

The first night he was slipping away from me. I knew he was dying— he could not he would not, I wouldn't let him. His miserable eyes looked up at me, and gradually they glazed over. I kept saying over and over, "You can't give up. Try. Damn it. Try. You must live. You must try to live. I love you." Gradually my voice lifted to an almost hysterical pitch as my hand clutched his shoulder with increasing intensity.

As Jack's eyes slowly stopped focusing, Dr. Schick leaned over and gently touched my arm. "It's no use. He can't hear you anymore." For one small moment I felt hate. He made me feel so foolish to be pushing a dying man. But I must make Jack very much want to live or he could never begin to rise above terribly weighted odds against him. As I looked up and saw the deep compassion within Dr. Schick's eyes, the feeling quickly subsided, and in its place I could only feel a great sense of gratitude.

My God, is this necessary? What a hell of a price we sometimes paid just to live. The chapel was not far away. The balcony was dark and a retreat from the harsh ceiling-lit glare of that ghastly intensive care unit with its never-ending stream of human tragedy. God was there in the chapel. He was really my friend. Sometimes I called him a nasty name. Sometimes I just told him I loved him. He was there. He quieted me when I was desperate and hysterical. He rested me when I felt I could not go on. He let me vent. He let me love. He let me hate. He knew he had asked terrible things of me. He had given me so many blessings.

The days blended into one endless effort to sustain Jack's life as he slipped back and forth from a conscious to semiconscious to comatose state and back again. At about the end of the third day, I begged Dr. Schick to try the Monaghan chest respirator. I was so sure, if only I could get that damn thing out of his mouth, I would be able to get orders from Jack as to what he was trying so hard to tell me. With his being able to say what was wrong, everything was going to start getting better. If I could just get him on the Monaghan, I thought I was reckoning with the fine thread that was the difference between whether he lived or died.

I hadn't bargained with the inadequacy of the Monaghan in ventilating someone with such a terrible loss of weight. Jack had become a mere skeletal figure. Dr. Schick had not used the Monaghan and was forced to rely on me for his knowledge of its ventilatory adequacy. That awful night! It was about eight in the evening. I had set up the Monaghan in the way I thought Jack had been using it at home. The bladder was inflated to seal off the dome, and face cloths were stuffed in the areas where there seemed to be air leaks. For a couple of hours it seemed to do an adequate job, so Dr. Schick pulled out the endotracheal tube. Jack seemed terribly relieved and promptly went to sleep.

At first I was thrilled, but before long the respirator started to indicate inadequate ventilation. Anxiety started to register again on Dr. Schick's face. How could this be? It seemed so right, this natural way of breathing. If only Jack would try a little harder. Where was God? Had he deserted me completely after going this far? The rushed, quietly controlled medical machine was already switching to high gear. *Call to see what doctors are in-house. Call Sister Rosemary, the head of the inhalation therapy department.* White uniforms started to move with a quickening pace. This must be serious, but Jack looked so peaceful. At first that particular look seemed deceptively peaceful. I was soon to learn the subtleties that indicated the difference between sleep and a comatose state.

There were no other doctors to intubate Jack at this hour of the night, and it had to be done immediately. Dr. Schick asked if I wished to stay. I said yes. The bed was quickly pulled away from the wall. I positioned myself next to Jack's head and held it in my hands. Dr. Schick quickly gloved and got the tube ready for insertion. Four or five hospital people hovered around, ready to help in any way they could. Once again the chest was lifted and the head held down as far as possible. Only this time I was holding the head. I was directed to and tried very hard to make a straight line of the passage for the tube to more easily pass down the throat.

It wasn't so easy. Once again the tube was being pushed fairly gently at first and then with increasing force as the situation grew more precarious. Dr. Schick's face had started out as collected as the first doctor on the first couple of tries. As the urgency increased, his anxiety was showing in faster almost darting movements, in the increased force used with the tube, in the shielded anxious eyes and taunt face. Orders were spit out in clipped, measured tones.

Once again the tube was coming back bloody. Jack's color, which had started as an unhealthy white with very little pink, changed to an angry red, then to a purple red, and finally to a whitish gray. I knew once again his chances of living were almost nonexistent. As I held his head in my hands, I nodded to one of the nurses, who quickly came over to take my position. Tears welled up once again as I quickly made my way to the chapel. This had to be it. The tube wasn't going down. An already emaciated and deathly sick body was being still further traumatized. Jack had already been several minutes without oxygen, and the tube still didn't seem as if it was about to go down. Sobs shook me as I waited in the quiet of the church balcony. A helpless grief possessed me. It tightened my chest and put my stomach in a knot. *Jack, how can you be so close and in a few minutes you will be so far away?*

It just could not be! *Damn it, God, where are you?* Then my mind filled with free-floating memories of the first day that our newborn baby John came home from the hospital. I was changing his diaper on the bed. I barely had his diaper off before he started urinating. Being a new mother and not expecting his piddling, I was leaning directly over him. Urine dripped off the end of my nose. Jack and I laughed uproariously. What about when we read in the paper at ten o'clock at night about a whale that had been washed ashore ninety miles away? Right away we put our three-month-old baby in the car to go see the whale. Now, even though he could no longer touch me physically, there was never a day that we didn't touch mentally. Life had been cruel, bringing upon us this awful affliction, but it had also brought us close together in so many ways.

How will the children take their father's death? How should I handle it? Should I try to make the burden as light as I can for them, or should I lean a little and let them share a great deal of my grief? Our son, John, in his quiet way had already moved his childhood Siamese cat to share his bedroom. Our daughter, Theresa, had moved the dog to her bedroom to keep her company at night. I couldn't believe this was happening. Never before had there been anything that I wanted so passionately that there wasn't some way of getting if I worked hard enough. He was the only one in the whole world with whom I had shared all kinds of mental explorations and private thoughts.

I felt so terribly alone. You can talk to God, but he doesn't answer you. You can talk to your kids, and even though they might very much want to help, they can only talk from the depths of their own needs. It takes so many years to build up that special something, a communion, between two people that quite often makes it possible for someone to say what is on the other person's mind before it comes out of their mouth.

The door behind me quietly opened, and a figure came down the few steps and sat beside me. Dr. Schick put his arm around me and gently said, "He is breathing now. We got the tube down." It couldn't be. He reassured me till finally I believed. He left. I had to talk to God again. *I'm sorry. I didn't mean to yell at you, but then I don't have to say I'm sorry. You already know. You are some great guy! Thanks! Thanks! I have to go now. Maybe he's conscious, and I know how he hates for me not to be there when he's conscious.*

Jack was in the hospital for several months before coming home. There were many crises of varying degrees. His body chemistry shifted constantly from overhydration to toxicity, his lungs couldn't clear mucus, his throat was raw from intubation, his skeleton arms were punctured with many needle marks, there was great difficulty in finding a new site to puncture, a Monaghan allowed far too much leakage to his almost skeletal frame, an iron lung resurrected from the hospital basement did not help further hydration, he developed infections with a high temperature, and he underwent ongoing medication checks with many variations, trying so hard to get longer-term positive results. Dr. Schick never faltered or ceased in his endless heroic efforts to save Jack's life. Jack died on May 23, 1976.

Chapter 11

Struggling

The following is a bitter haunting memory of love's refrain. *Jack, you will never touch me again.* I've said it. The words seared into a memorandum of torturous reality. *You will never reach over in our bed to run your fingers down my face. You will never caress me as you throb with desire. I feel so bleak. We had our differences. You could be a cruel bastard. You were always in command. We were two people searching for some unknown something. We each had what the other needed, but we were too psychologically naive to be able to take advantage of that fact. You have always been so strong. Maybe it was your downfall physically. What a torturous load you carried. Were our sights set too high? Searching for a PhD took its ugly toll. The awful drive we both had. We must make it, but make what?*

In the days before you knew the kind of stuff I was made of, and even for many years after, you would never lean on me, even in times of your near death. Finally somehow it got across to you with the long hospitalization how much I really loved you. Damn it. It's about time that God, my friend, pulls another rabbit out of the hat. What the hell is he waiting for?

Jack, if you really tried, couldn't you move just a little? Damn it. Try. I know you have tried, and I know you keep trying, but I can't help hating you a little along with loving you for making me suffer so. Don't you know how much I care? You've found a way to do everything else. Damn it. Find a way to move.

If only I could do something like give you a kidney. I feel as if I personally willed you to live through those four weeks in the hospital. I forced you. I pulled, cajoled, and threatened you and God alike.

It's as if somehow I've managed to get everything I've always really wanted in life, but no matter how I twist with this one, it's to no avail. My head is bloodied, my fingers are torn and raw, and my heart is bleeding, but I cannot make a dent. Why is this so? God, are you mocking me? You're so damn smart. Why don't you let go with a little more generosity that you've been so good with up to this time? Why won't you do this one thing for me? Sometimes you seem so close, and other times you just don't seem to be around at all.

After Jack's four-week hospitalization and he was home again, I asked him if he would have chosen to die in the hospital when his heart had stopped and before he was resuscitated. He answered, "Yes."

Chapter 12

Little Flower Nursing Home: 1971–1975

The welts were rising on my bruised flesh. I was thoroughly desolated. In a death grip of distraught anxiety, desperately trying to hold back tears, I let my assistant, Irene Carman, the brilliant woman who helped me through so many dark hours, and the food service manager, Adeline Peck, be pummeled and spat upon without rescuing them from their 1199 Union tormentors.

Their games were such ugly ones. If anything extra was to be asked of the employees, the union must demonstrate to their members a method of their getting a pound of flesh. The methods were always frontal attacks carried out in a manner most suitable for the moment. The initial attack was always against the owner. He or she was always identified as a "thief" in one way or another. The word was used over and over referring to my husband Jack's first contacts with Union 307 as the possible union to represent the employees at the Little Flower Nursing Home.

Union organizer Eddie Kay picked up speed. "You were dishonest with June Fisher. You only mentioned temporary and probation employees. You didn't mention anything about your part-timers. What do you think we are, fools?" As Kay threw out his rapier remarks, Israel, another union organizer who accompanied him, let out ugly laughs and then threw in nasty, stinging addendums. The show went on hour after hour with ongoing jabbing reminders that administration must be cut.

I had asked the New York State Department of Health for approval of the number of employees considered adequate for patient care in order to have subsequent costs covered under Medicaid rates that would be promulgated by the department. With all of my talk of possible staff cuts, where I ended up with a little better than one-half of what I had asked for from the Department of Health, the ugly remarks that had just been passed were just a taste of what was to come. When Eddie Kay had seen me fairly easily moved to tears, he moved his major insults to include Carman and Peck. He then encouraged the two Little Flower Nursing Home union delegates, Betty Siegel from dietary and June Ford from nursing, to move into attack mode as he directed an orgiastic, ventilating, venomous barrage of words upon the two supervisors.

I could fight a clean fight. I could fight dirty fights. But fighting with my hands tied behind my back was deadly. Did I kick? Did I scream? Did I stare hate? Did I respond with the same venom? I had no time to evaluate as I went along. My back was constantly being put against the wall. By the time I was given the bottom line, Mr. Reir, my lawyer, had long since gone home. Kay was working on buffeting and pummeling me into accepting his latest demands. Should I have accepted? Should I have fought his ultimatum that he said in his thunderous, leering, threatening tone? "Accept what I'm giving you or take a strike."

It would take me days to try to evaluate the monetary and psychological fallout of the terms that I'd been forced to take. Even on reevaluation I didn't know whether my personal responses were correct, as they pertained only to me. Many employees were present through many of Kay's harangues and Israel's mocking ugliness. What they took away with them was extremely difficult but important for me to weigh as the day progressed. Early during this siege I had decided I would allow Kay a frontal attack on myself with only a fairly passive demeanor. As the day progressed, somehow my tears on several occasions had elicited some favorable responses from union employees.

Noting same Kay's attacks changed. I wasn't emotionally prepared and failed to change my response as the attacks were redirected to others. Kay's attacks were made with fine precision. He found Mrs. Carmen's acute pain threshold was reached with the word "fuck." He pounced on this with glee. He jabbed out the word over and over as the conversation immediately became a screaming match. He quickly thrust the word in sentence after sentence. When she abruptly left after his ultimate hurtful "Fuck you," he almost instantly changed back to a quiet demeanor.

There was only one thing of which I was very sure—I should have had Mrs. Carman leave the room after Kay used foul words in his attack on her. The only thing that I had left to tell myself and her was that I did the very best that I could at the time and hopefully that would be good enough for both her and myself to live with. I prayed that this would be so. My soul was bare. It was one thirty in the morning. I wished to weep no more.

The amount of pressure I got at work and my reaction to it were directly related to Jack's response. When the wolves were getting in their nipping and biting, he became a concerned and compassionate person, but as soon as the pressure let up a little at the nursing home, he added pressure with a casual dropping of "Did you do this or that?" and we were off and running once again.

Would the lions ever stop chasing their tails? Would the carousel never stop its contortions of movement and sound? Could I ever get off, or must I fall off into a bottomless pit?

I must understand where my insecurity came from and why it stayed with me for all of these years. Why did I still feel a choking sensation of bitter loss with his rejection, which was absolutely inevitable after a wasted exchange? He didn't understand, and I wasn't sure that he wanted to. His inevitable response to a quarrel was always the final one of rejection. He felt his own pain. Did he try to understand mine? Whether I was right or wrong, it didn't matter. The end of all quarrels was almost always the same torturous rejection. It was what made me react so violently. I knew that whether I was right or wrong, he might end up apologizing later. If I could make myself stay away long enough, the result of the initial quarrel would be rejection. It's been honed down to a scathing final "go home" accompanied by a look of pure hate or "go home" with averted eyes.

I tried so hard to not make it important if he told me he knew how hard I was working and that I was doing a good job. I still couldn't even begin to understand how it could be so damn important to me. If he even turned his own head or moved a little finger, I was an emotional cripple with an intolerable dependency. He still managed to weave and connive to make me dance on a string.

Every time I began to feel as if I had taken steps away from his emotional support with a degree of assurance I'd be like someone who has wandered a little way out of the womb of psychological support. First, it was only one or two steps that I took away from the mouth of the cave before my rope ran out and I was brutally dragged back within the shadow of my needs. Every time I reassured myself, "I can do it. I must do it. The rope is literally killing me." My steps were a few more, my rope may be a little thinner and longer, but the effect was still devastatingly similar. I was pulled back to my cave over and over again. I didn't know if I would ever be free. Could I survive alone? Would I always have the need for a psychological crutch no matter what the price was or even if it killed me?

I stood alone. There wasn't as yet a deadly struggle to pay bills. I had no struggle for breath. There was only the never-ending running and groping from one day to the next to desperately try to do enough to keep the baying pack of wolves from being able to get hold of my heels. How long could I continue? Did I want to even try? Who cared? Everyone was so involved with themselves. No one could see any blood.

Thanks to that damn New England ethical code, verbalizing psychological pain in our society was an indication of an inherent weakness. People only understood what they could see. Even if I tried to make someone understand, it always ended up with my half-apologizing for mentioning my feelings. By the time, my understanding that I'm feeling pangs of guilt for talking of my psychological needs in light of Jack's, at least visually much greater needs, frequently leaves me with a shrill defensive nagging self-pitying verbalization which infuriates me and around I go again.

The furious battle was on with me, as well as with Jack, as I tried to maintain my self-image while I was caught in a web of never-ending shifting emotions. He would not release me, and I could not seem to free myself.

Chapter 13

Words to Disabled Husband Jack

I feel so sad. I want to be with you. I want to make those sad eyes dance in my presence. He was retreating, as he had so many times before. It was as if I couldn't make an all-out effort anymore. *Oh, damn it to hell. Why does it have to be like this? It's like watching a sinking ship and you're all played out. You're finding it more and more difficult to keep throwing me a lifeline. Oh hell, why? Why? We could really be good together, and you're leaving me.*

His eyes were getting distant and slightly tinged with hate in their retreating silence. The slim line between us was growing taut and still daring itself to be tested. Would it stand up to much more strain? We loved, we hated, and now this. Oh God, how I tried. If he retreated now, I couldn't stand the way I was living. The small element of happiness that I seemed to bring him was what made my life bearable, and now this.

I was afraid. I felt myself rejected. It was as though I must also withdraw to protect myself from what? I wasn't sure. *I no longer seem to be able to touch you. It's as if the stark inhumanity of your lifestyle is finally draining away the verbal and physical touching that we have been doing for the last twelve years. Must it end this way? Must you become a robot? Is it the only way you can live? I am frightened. Even as I talk to you of the children or the horses or the business, your responses are cold and flat. We've been through so much. Don't leave me now. I love you.*

It's as though you have willed an emotional island where no one can intrude, not even me. Why? Has your fear preordained this emotional death so that you would be prepared for what you think has to be my final withdrawal? Can't you accept things the way they were? How can you possibly think that this is better? You are tormenting me. It was such a short time ago that you were sad when I was sad, and I was sad when you were sad. Now it seems to be only me who so heavily feels your moods. Why? Have you lost your capacity to love? Don't you need me anymore?

Chapter 14

Jack Santmann

Theresa was dividing her time between 146 No. Carll Avenue and where their children, John and Theresa, lived at 66 Cedar Lane in Babylon. Theresa called Jack on the phone. "I can't sleep. I'm worried about everything. How am I going to make the payments on the house, pay the taxes, the employees' salaries, etc.? What I said last night was nothing, and you reacted so negatively by not looking at me and not talking." Jack responded, "You're crazy about the money. I'll explain it tomorrow." He hung up and called back a little later. "Do you want to come over?"

Theresa said, "Yes."

There was a long discussion between Theresa and Jack at 146 North Carll Avenue.

Jack said, "I don't have the guts to commit suicide. I don't want to live, but I don't have the guts to commit suicide. If there ever was a time to die, this is it."

"I don't want you to die. I'm dependent on you."

"I know that, but why?"

Theresa said, "I don't know."

"I wouldn't say anything if you got yourself a boyfriend. Would that help? Have you ever had one?"

"No. If I did get a boyfriend, you wouldn't be able to look at me."

Jack said, "Yes, that's true. I can take what is happening to me, but I can't take what I'm doing to you. I just can't take that anymore. What are we going to do? I know you are depressed and very lonely. I don't think you have ever tried to make female friends."

Theresa replied, "You already know what happens. What would you like me to talk about, kids or recipes? I can't, and you know that even if I could, five or ten female friends are not the same as one male friend."

Jack asked, "Why don't you just leave me? You would get over me in a month or two."

"I can't. If I could, I probably would have been gone a long time ago. I am dependent on you. I don't know why. It's like you're part of me. I feel such empathy."

Jack said, "I feel the same way about you. Is there anything I can do to help?"

"No. Why do you, when you get furious at something I say, just completely turn away? You won't speak. You won't look at me. You just tell me to get out as I plead, scream, rant and rave, apologize, and throw a tantrum for two days before you talk to me again. If you have such empathy, how can you do that to me?"

"I don't know."

Theresa continued, "Yesterday it was nothing. I would rather not discuss the way I felt on Saturday night. I have that right, and you instantly got so furious you wouldn't even look at me."

"I interpreted it as hostile and angry."

"How could you? I can't imagine interpreting your saying in a quiet tone that you would rather not discuss anything at any one time as hostile. It makes me recoil with terror at your moving to the Little Flower Nursing Home. I can't say anything about anything that displeases me without your interpreting it as hostile."

Theresa feared Jack's move to the Little Flower Nursing Home even though a room next to the administrator's office had been set up for him with a piped-in oxygen line and a direct line to the nursing station on the first floor. The back area of the second floor had been built to accommodate his wife, Theresa, and their children, John and Theresa. The very aggressive and often hostile Union 1199 had quickly infiltrated the staff of the nursing home soon after its opening in October 1993. She had been told by the nonunion staff that the union staff had let it be known that they were not going to incorporate floor duties with his care. Every nurse's aide and LPN and many RNs were in the union, which presented Theresa with insurmountable problems.

Jack said, "I'm sorry if I took it the wrong way. What are you going to do when Theresa leaves home?"

Theresa replied, "I don't know. Well, I'd better get some sleep. I love you."

Jack, very quietly, responded, "I know, that's the trouble."

Most of the time I felt like crying. Why was he so damn cold? No matter how good I felt when I went to see him after work, I always came away feeling torn apart and on the verge of tears. How could a man who needed help to take every single breath have such an element of control over me? Was it because of a basic weakness of mine? Could I ever be free? Would I go on till I died, struggling with my psychological dependence on a voice that made such demands of me? I tried every trick I knew with myself. Did I enjoy being tormented? How in hell could he still have such control over my very soul? My self-worth somehow seemed to be tied up to the little innuendos of a slightly raised eyebrow. Good God, he could hardly raise the eyebrow, and here I was saying how important it was to me. Was he my penance to attain heaven? He was my psychological well-being and my hell. I couldn't understand. I struggled as one against chains, but then I was not sure I was in chains. Rather, I was enmeshed in a shadowy, foggy, shifting spiderweb of constantly changing nuances. Shades of darkness would alternate with shades of light. Was I just managing to slip through life without its being killingly abrasive?

It went on and on. This must come to an end, but it never did. I reached out, and there was no one there. With all of Jack's horrendous problems, he still in some inconceivable way was my tiny island. The water lapped at my feet; the storm raged around me. The sky was frequently filled with never-ending strife of jagged lightning and angry dark-gray clouds, only relieved on occasion by glimpses of a rather light but very pure intense blue. The waves would wash me, or I would drown! Why was I staying here? Where could I go? What were my options? I didn't think I had any. Maybe I was Cleopatra's Needle. I would last forever. The storms raged on and on. I had feelings inside that would never be free. I could scream out, I could rant and rave, but I would continue to stand and the storm would go on and on and on. Jack suggested I take medication.

My answer was "Never."

The days were wearing on, and his mental condition was such a god-awful thing to bear. But if it was difficult for me, it was obviously excruciatingly difficult for him. Last night, on March 25, 1976, when I went to see him, his verbalization was extremely brief. "What happened today?" I asked while I was telling him he was maintaining a semi-attentive stare.

A few moments later he said, "I don't feel like talking." His eyes fixed on a distant place in the room. Pure misery reflected in those trapped eyes as tears solely gathered and the rims reddened.

Must this go on forever? Yesterday he was going to take over the drug business for the nursing home, and today he was in the pits of hell.

About two months ago I came home from a two-day trip to find a Levin tube protruding from Jack's nostril. There was instant alarm. Why this added intrusion? First there was the mouth respirator fifteen years ago. Five years ago it was the chest respirator. Then four years ago with the deadly hospital siege came the tracheotomy. Now came the final indignity of the Levin tube coming out of his nose and winding around his face. There was that monster fear. His talking had been affected by the constant suctioning, sometimes every five minutes, to clear his chest and oral secretions. Fear seemed to be tightening the esophagus. He was displaying unbearable wretched panic. "What do I do?" His words were barely audible. If the tube was pulled, he would starve to death. If the tube stayed in, he couldn't breathe. I blocked out of my memory bank what happened next.

Chapter 15

Attacks

It was March 28, 1976. *Are you a harsh taskmaster and selfish tyrant or a brave, loving, loyal husband?* And life went on. Only a few weeks ago brought the dreaded Levin tube. Jack had been slowly starving for over three and a half years until his shiny skin just hung over protruding cheekbones. Usually a beard hid some of the harshness of the sunken cheeks and sometimes partially hid the neck that was little more than a stick holding up the remains of his head. His eyes were the only detection of his mood. In them many reflections poured forth in such a few moments. More and more, the protruding eyes told instantly of compelling fear or the slightly narrowed, drawn, despair-ridden, long drawn out daily fear. Other times it was the look of hate and hostility with averted eyes that only very briefly flitted over me to then stare at any other part of the room. Sometimes there was an accusing, penetrating stare of utter contempt. Other times it was a look of love.

Where was that man who kept me in utter control in tearful sympathy with his almost constant despair? I had given up. I used to make feeble attempts with self-control. I went to Virginia for about two days some twelve years ago. I never intended to stay. Jack's smiles and sparkling eyes appeared so seldom and were so precious to me. His rejections had been hideously cruel and complete. "Leave the room, go away, or I'm going to the hospital." Our doctor had called a top hospital in Massachusetts for a consultation. The hospital seemed to be intrigued with the possibility of further study of Jack's condition, as the diagnosis of ALS was to some extent speculative. They had offered to have him go to their hospital for a free stay while he was being studied. Even in his terribly compromised situation, I felt panic over the thought of his leaving me.

There were screaming attacks and counterattacks. It had been over twenty years, and I'd come to the conclusion that I could never leave him. I could not stand the thought of the consequences. He probably would die right away and then not only would I have to live with myself but even worse society pointing at me as having done in a brave courageous man who by sheer willpower and guts gave me everything I owned. I couldn't live the balance of my life with the possible pointing of fingers, where I would have enough self-doubt to never be free till I was dead. So whatever happened, as long as Jack was alive, I would be his wife.

Any acceptance from Jack was being very carefully rationed out in stingy little fragments or not at all. An outright question searching for praise after a supreme effort was likely to get at best "That was a good job."

As soon as I got to 146 North Carll Avenue, my day usually started with Jack's reminding me to do certain chores of one kind or other. My workday had almost never been less than eight hours and frequently many more. My feeling was usually one of instant, intense anger. I knew the route all too well. He pushed the buttons, and I had to jump. I didn't really care whether the interest in the reserve fund went to the nursing home or to us. Jack reassured me that the money in the reserve fund escrow was ours, as we were paying income taxes on it. It was April 19, 1976, and I was burdened now by grotesquely important heavy-pressure items, including the last of the audit going on at the nursing home. I had to try to understand more before he left. The nursing home report was being sent to Albany, which would affect the rate for 87 percent of the patients. The entire kitchen must be quickly revamped to go from china to paper. There was an ongoing breaking of dishes and the sabotage of equipment by my 1,199 employees. There would have to be layoffs with the ever-hanging threat of a strike. There was the letter from the New York State Health Department on my cutting staff and if my nursing hours of direct patient care were sufficient. I must do a study to answer the question. Medicare papers must be filed before the end of the month, along with dozens of pages of an HE2 document that would go to the health department in Albany, which also affected the Medicaid rate. Would the pressure never cease? It always seemed to be there no matter what I said or did. If it wasn't the damn interest, it was something else. It wasn't said like "Do you have time now?" It was just a dropped "It needs to be done." The interest question had already been mentioned four or five times. *Jesus, I don't give a damn. Leave me alone. Stop hassling me. Instead say, "I understand how much work you're doing." Just any damn thing but that continuing persistent dropping of what has to be done.* I was furious. My anger was never understood. It was just another of the castigating ever-loving things that I hated that I must accept like a damn lap dog to be accepted and loved.

Could I never be free? Could I ever accept the fact that the only way I could have a semblance of peace was to break these chains that bound me? But I must know the chains if I was ever to break them. I didn't know this until the last week or two. I had made a feeble attempt to psychologically free myself, but I couldn't and now I knew I would not.

God, help us all!

Jack's words were frequently terrible, brutal, and cold. The eyes got narrow and mean. As best he could he fairly hissed, "I have a problem and you have to help me solve it. I want you to hire three nurse's aides at the nursing home who will work for me two days a week. You don't want to do it only for personal preference. Then you solve my staffing problems. The problem is all yours. Go ahead. It's all yours. I have been trying to solve it for over a year, and you veto everything. I'm not going to the nursing home. I'm not wanted, and I'm not going." Next came his pleading and cajoling. He said, "I don't think anything would be different over there. I would see less of you and Theresa than I do now." How tortured, and how torturing. I had been forcing my love on him for years. He contorted and twisted so much of what I said. It would take screaming tirades, tears, and cajoling to manipulate the words back into their proper perspective. What would I have been like under his circumstances? Would I have made like demands to maintain my sanity as a quadriplegic for so many years? I wonder if he would have been around that many years later, as I was.

There was now such an awful struggle for life. It went on through suctioning every five minutes till trickles of bright-red blood ran in the Levin tube, through turning of his head, putting the respirator's mouthpiece at a different angle, turning the chest respirator up and down, through bedpans and urinals, legs up or down, hands up or down, tube feedings, face washes, nose blowing, arms by his side or on top of the chest respirator, and the Monaghan turned up for deep breathing or down far enough to try to talk without so much air that he couldn't make the machine shut off in order to talk. What now happened most of all? Repeat, repeat, repeat. The words were coming out as those of someone with a very severe cleft palate. When he was upset, nothing came out. He mouthed, "I'm not afraid to die. I'm just afraid to live and not be able to talk. Then what will I do? I'm so afraid to live. I'm a coward. I can't die." I reassured him, "Never, ever can you do anything that would label you a coward. You have proved that you are courageous beyond words." I cajoled and pleaded and poured out love.

Sometimes if I was desperate and hated him in answer to some of his ugly prods, I had to control myself. The bitter depths of the pit where people seemed to search for the ugliest words of recrimination and hate were so destructive to the perpetrator, as well as the recipient. Psychologically he was constantly devastating me. About two months ago I had finally answered for myself why he had such a powerful hold on me. I knew he had never loved anyone as he had me.

No matter where I turned, it kept cropping up. Death was like a many-headed monster. Chop off one head, one threat of death, and two days later another head, another face, was leering at me. I was on a seemingly never-ending death watch.

There were never-ending frantic calls. At eleven o'clock at night on Sunday, May 9, 1976, blood was coming from suctioning and had been all afternoon. There were frustrations of Jack's noncompliance with my previous findings and doctor's orders. Two weeks before, I told him of the consistency of the most recent suction catheters, which the doctor had ordered. They were much more rigid than the ones that he had used previously. I had warned him that they would cause damage if used too frequently. He had been suctioned every few minutes for hours. The back of his throat on the other side of his trach button had become traumatized and was bleeding. One-third of the suction bottle was filled with the rich crimson color of blood. He was frantic. "I must be suctioned to breathe." If he continued to be suctioned, he would continue to bleed. He was angry and insisted that I give him an answer. He looked at me with a mixture of terror, anger, and pleading. Finally, after several hours, his being kept at a forty-five-degree angle seemed to ease the secretions and bleeding. I went home. Several hours later I was called back. He had the catheters boiled to soften them. His blood had gone down to the area of his lungs and clotted. On suctioning, large clots were blocking the catheter. The same problem was still looming. If there was too much of the in and out of suctioning, he would start to bleed again. If the accumulated blood was not suctioned out, he couldn't breathe. It was finally settled that we would do more suctioning to bring up clots. But I blocked out of my mind what came next.

Chapter 16

Coming to Terms with Death

It was May 13, 1976. He let me vent my anger, and then I struggled once more to hear his words "I love you, I shall always love you" and then a strong "Live, live." *My God, what am I doing? I must change instantly.* The awful specter of possibly having cruel words be the last words from me to him after all these years would be a horrid burden to bear. During the time before his death was so close, when he had been so demanding, impatient, and sometimes so verbally cruel, all the frustrations and anger of the past years came seething to the top. Now all of my anger had subsided.

All I could think of was the tremendous joy when he arrived home from work to our New York City apartment; the way he made me feel like the prettiest, sexiest woman in the world; how he took such pleasure in buying me whatever he could manage; the pleasure he took in our children; the pleasure he took in my being happy driving in the car with the window down, whether it was summer or winter; how he let me talk him into so many things, such as going to see his father, whom he hadn't seen in many years; his enjoyment of squashy love notes when he was away for a few hours; his concern over sick kids; his pride in my accomplishments in school and business; his pride in the way I looked; his letting me have a kitten in our Manhattan apartment and spending money we couldn't really afford; our joy over three hundred dollars in cash (we threw it in the air, and it fell all over the floor as we gleefully saw for the first time that much money in cash at one time); and our first rug (we practically slept on it the first night, we were so thrilled)—it was the small white rug with red roses, which he let me buy just for decoration even though we couldn't afford it.

The following is something I wrote for Jack several weeks before his death:

All the things I want to thank you for: your grave tender concerns during son John's convulsions; your gentle support during labor pains; never wanting to be away from me from the very beginning of the marriage; joy at the children's first words and first steps; giving me the side of the bed I wanted; having the same dollar sense that I do; never having a problem with religion and leaving mine up to me; loving my country; taking me crabbing in a rowboat with fresh stitches from a hernia operation; buying me a breast pump when I got hysterical about an underfed child even though it wasn't true; getting me linens from the youth house; holding three jobs while going for your PhD; being as glad to see me and John as we were to see you when you got off the elevator; going back for my basketball trophy, which you had used to break open the fire escape window when we had a fire; jumping to my defense when I got in a fight; always being loyal when talking about me to other people; rarely complaining about your condition; our building the nursing home; your bravery and courage against unbelievable odds; taking all possible burdens from me for as long as you had breath; and most of all, loving me forever.

For your telling me how good my writing is; doing term papers for me; using the same toothbrush if one of us forgot ours; letting me buy my mother gifts, with no reluctance when we couldn't afford to, even though you didn't like her; never complaining about my housekeeping; complimenting me on my child rearing; being tidy around the house; being very ambitious; being meticulous about your person;

thinking I was lovely when I was pregnant; never being upset with animals I loved; liking my cooking; holding my hand psychologically when you couldn't anymore physically; being a good provider; always doing your best; not making it obvious when you looked at other women; and letting me know that I was the only true love you ever had and then telling me in many little ways that this was true.

For loving to do crazy things, like going to the shore eighty miles away at ten o'clock at night with a three-month-old kid to see a whale that had washed up on the beach even though you had to go to work the next day; liking the same movies I did; being the father of my children; buying me the house I loved when we shouldn't have; encouraging flying and scuba diving lessons; liking my friend Helen; and sharing so much beauty and joy with me—a sleeping child, a toothless grin, a rising sun, a good report card, and a successful business meeting.

For wanting to share everything with me; leaning on me, as well as supporting me; being so independent and so very strong about everything except being without me; sending me away to be with Theresa even though I know you very much wanted me to stay; being my psychological strength for all these years; understanding the dichotomy of my bold front and my shy inner self; never failing me when I needed to borrow your strength; when you didn't have the answers, doing the research that got the answers; allowing me to separate your care from our relationship; working so terribly hard all these years; and most of all, loving me forever.

For loving our children; having almost no disagreements on how to raise them; always remembering the special events with gifts; hating to see me cry; telling me that even during our bitterest fights you never stopped loving me for one moment; and getting angry and happy over almost all of the same things I did.

Jack's tears slowly ran down his face as I read the words above. He died on May 23, 1976.

Chapter 17

Death Watch

It was May 17, 1976. Would this death watch never end? The three trees at the north side of the house had pushed skyward their offerings of armfuls of fragile pink petals and then, overladen with their ethereal loveliness, had gradually let them fall gently to the ground. Four years ago, with their first stirring of promise in April, I had followed Jack to the hospital. I had agonized with the daily life-and-death struggle as the trees laden with blossoms had come out with all their promise. I had not been betrayed. He lived.

This time it was different. Jack's eyes were finally resigned. He was going to die. There no longer was the angry, terrified panic of only a couple of weeks ago. His voice was fading, which was his last thin and unsteady lifeline. He was totally incapacitated, with some degree of breathing impairment. He could still give orders to keep himself alive, but now his voice was going. Now what?

There were so many damn stupid remarks that people made, like "Everyone has a right to live." What on God's earth of the right to die? What of peace? We all so desperately sought peace, and here was daily agonizing—his and mine.

For years I had chased one hope after another—Yale Medical School, Mount Sinai Hospital, and Columbia Presbyterian Medical Center. For several years, twice weekly I took him to a New Jersey hospital for electrical stimulation. I located a place in Florida where snake venom was sold and made a trip to Florida to get a vial. We tried hypnosis, concentrated vitamins, prolonged antibiotic gentamicin injections, and truth serum.

I loved him. I truly did. I had pleaded, screamed, and cajoled. There was no more life.

He was cruel. "When will you get it through your head I can't help you anymore?" His words cut quick and deep. My response was the same as that of many years ago—instant furious anger—but for the first time he didn't respond in anger. He then went on to help me with my questions, and then he fell back into quiet helplessness.

At six o'clock in the evening on May 23, 1976, Jack died. A lonely voice cried out, "Where are you? Can you care? Can you see? Can you touch? Are you walking? Are you running? Is your mother finally a comfort? Wherever you are, are you saying, as you did last week, 'I shall love you forever'? I have no feeling but love.

"Are you with me now? Shall you finally live with me in this fine house that I love so much? As your body lies white and terribly wasted, are you free at last?

"God, you were my friend before. Touch him now. Please let him be free."

Chapter 18

I Miss Him

It was June 15, 1976. I missed him. It had been almost a month since his death. Trying to straighten out a myriad of problems had kept me from sinking into an abyss, but great waves of feelings of a deep personal loss washed over me as I drove to and from work. When something special had happened and he was the only one who really cared very deeply, I was comforted. Now, as I had no one to talk to, I kept seeing his face. Sometimes the eyes were sparkling with a Cheshire cat look, and other times they carried the misery of the world. I chided myself a few times about my regrets (*If only I had done this or that*). I felt a deep ache of loneliness.

The questions haunted me. Could he see? Could he feel? Did he know I was thinking of him? Did he want to touch me? I looked for signs. Three very large bushes that a maintenance man had mutilated went through spring with only one or two tiny signs of life. Since Jack's death, they had shown much more life.

The cemetery was close by. I hadn't gone to visit the grave. Did he mind? He worked so damn hard to live. The last three or four months were consumed with a desperate struggle to get nourishment down his Levin tube and to aerate his lungs. His struggle for life was frequently reflected in cold, brittle commands. His eyes, when not reflecting agony or a very infrequent twinkle, were always analytical. He was very bright. He quickly analyzed material from accountants, lawyers, and doctors. He then plotted the information into a course of action.

Did he fear death, or did he just have a burning desire to live? He wanted so desperately to live, but how could it be so under such incredibly stressful conditions? Added to his physical condition were many stressful circumstances, such as employees arguing for almost an hour that they were going to quit if he made one of them work a certain day, even though the one scheduled to work had called in sick. Another time they were verbalizing to him about trying to go union and asked, "What will we do if you die?" They had heard about the 1199 Union at the Little Flower Nursing Home. In addition, I had heard squeaky noises from the union at the Little Flower Nursing Home about possibly unionizing the Little Flower Residence. The income at the residence could not begin to support a union shop. The employees from the residence traveled across the street to take care of Jack at 146 North Carll Avenue when he called them over by intercom or shortwave radio. There was no money and absolutely no way to support a staff exclusively for him. The whole thing was a wretched nightmare. When he told me of such exchanges, his eyes were apologizing pools of torment. "I know you have a lot of problems with the union and the health department, but I just have to talk to someone and there isn't anybody else. I can't hold it in anymore." At times like these, bitter feelings of pure hate choked me. I was caught in a web of the dregs of human reaction in the face of tormented human needs. It would be easy to fall into an abyss of hostile negativism toward humanity, but what of all the moments of concern that have come through from others?

I tried to live with the thought that all of us did the best that we could. Few of us indeed choose not to be liked or to use our attributes to maximal advantage, though sometimes the lines sure got hazy as to whom the maximum advantage of a situation would primarily be for—family, self, peers, or others.

It was June 27, 1976. The great waves of loneliness that had washed over me since Jack's death had finally begun to ease. It was as if a vital part of me had died. Tears were always trying to come out, but when it was the time of day that I could afford the luxury of crying, tears usually did not come. Driving a car, especially going back and forth to the nursing home, had been a time of great sorrow. The feeling of loss was particularly intense.

Chapter 19

Mother and Daughter

The following were my general observations for Munich, Germany; London, England; Amsterdam, Holland; Brussels, Belgium; Strasbourg, France; and Luxembourg and Schaffhausen in Northern Switzerland. There were no screens in the windows. There were very few flies or bugs of any kind. Germany's cars were bigger than those of other countries. All of the cemeteries that I saw abounded with multicolored, well-tended flowers. There were quite a few small bedroom trailers being used.

Hertz Rent-a-Car was very expensive. Budget and Avis were less expensive and similar in cost. In Amsterdam I rented the only car available, a small stick shift for about $150 with unlimited mileage for one week plus gas. We got in the car. I tried to find something that might resemble a brake and could find none. I was jerking my way down the street when I finally got information concerning the location of the brake from a man walking on the side of the road. Terry drove in Belgium and Germany.

We bought food at supermarkets or small grocery stores. We had fresh fruit and bread. Some containers had the native language on their wrapping, so we shook them, trying to figure out if we were actually purchasing milk. In most of the countries there were very few people who spoke English. In one grocery store I saw the universal sign for a restroom. After I had entered the stall, I had no more than pulled down my underwear and squatted when I looked up, and much to my embarrassment there was a man looking down at me. That seemed to be very much the norm in European countries.

There were many banks where we exchanged US money for the currency of the countries visited. Most restaurants and hotels accepted traveler's checks, American Express, and US dollars. We were told to look for favorable rates of exchange for American money and to carry some small denominations in traveler's checks, such as three hundred dollars in twenties, a few fifties, and the rest in hundreds.

My plan for hotel accommodations was to have Terry follow our travels on a map and choose a city that we would get to at approximately six or seven o'clock in the evening, at which time we would almost certainly be able to get a hotel room for the night. We never had any problems driving into a city, looking for a fairly nice hotel, and getting quite acceptable rooms with a shower or bath. If I asked for a room that was quiet and off the street with a shower, I was likely to pay less, as well as have a smaller room and only a shower rather than a tub and shower.

In all of the countries we visited, hand harvesting was utilized such as a sickle for cutting corn. In Germany, small tractors were coming and going in the fields for harvesting crops and taking manure from the barns to the fields, etc.

London had what was called instant fare available to Amsterdam for one-half of the regular fare of thirty-seven pounds versus sixty-six pounds, with the caveat that it had to be for a round trip. KLM had a much more limited number of flights on instant fare than British Airways. KLM reservations had to be made the same morning of the flight, while British Airways let us make reservations the night before.

It was probably the same in other countries, as well as Amsterdam. If a car was left in a country other than the one in which it was rented, there was an extra charge of approximately forty-five dollars for a small sedan and sixty-five dollars for a Mercedes.

The Germans were strong, industrious, and friendly people. No one understood English. There were many small crucifixes on the side of the road. There was a cemetery with very colorful flower arrangements among tombstone markers, some with small wooden crosses dating back to the 1930s.

We stopped at a barn house in the middle of a village through which we were traveling. I wanted to see up close what farm living looked like in Germany. Terry was reluctant and gingerly followed me into the barn. An elderly woman came and greeted us with such warmth, as if we were welcome relatives who had stopped by for a visit. She did not understand any English, so she fetched a young daughter who understood a bit of English.

We watched eight or nine cows being milked by an electric milking machine. A goat in the rear portion of the barn had babies only three days old that we were welcomed to hold. There were three small pigs in a six-by-eight-foot pen and a very large pig in another pen of the same size. The large pig's pen was about four feet from the door that opened into the kitchen of the house. A sign near the road read "Zimmer." I thought it meant "bed and breakfast," but the girl had disappeared sometime before we left so I didn't have anyone to ask. To this day I am sorry I didn't pursue a possible overnight stay at a German farmhouse.

There were both government-run and private hospitals. The national health insurance premium was forty dollars per month.

On August 20, 1976, my daughter, Theresa, and I flew from the United States to London, England, to start our two-week vacation in Europe. In London, I bought instant fare for a round trip to Amsterdam and back to London for half the regular fare. The exchange rate was one pound equaled $1.82 to $1.86. While in London we stayed at the Mayfair Hotel for fifty-five dollars a day for two with twin beds.

In Amsterdam, Holland, we stayed at the Krasnapolsky for 109 guilders for two with twin beds and no bath. A room with a bath was 136 guilders. A breakfast of ham, cheese, assorted breads, and coffee came with the room. On dollar equaled 2.68 guilders. We were told it was the warmest it had been in 450 years. Amsterdam was noted for diamonds and canals. I rented a small Volkswagen stick shift for $150.55 week, plus $10.20 per km. Swedish plates were on the car, so we would leave it in Switzerland and not have a one-way rental charge, because that was the country we would be flying out of. There were no automatics available anywhere. It turned out great, as there were no problems with the stick shift, and the manual was less than half the price of an automatic.

We took canal rides, and we could see through many houses on the first floor when the curtains were not drawn. Our German seatmate explained that the custom evolved many years ago. It was obvious that no commercial business was going on in the homes, which assured lower taxes. At the peak of the roof were pulleys for getting furniture in the houses through windows, because doorways were too narrow. Legal and illegal houseboats, from small to large and of every possible description, were in the thousands. Some were shanties. Most of them had flowers beautifully arranged and growing around their exteriors. There were no screens on the windows. Almost everyone spoke English, which was a pleasant surprise.

Drugs abounded in Amsterdam. We were very close to a drug bust. A policeman had taken a needle out of the hand of a young man, who he had spread-eagled over a car. The man was being charged with purse snatching.

We drove from Amsterdam through the Dutch countryside. Farms, as well as huge areas of greenhouses, abounded. Cows and sheep were everywhere. Where industry villages and farms met was abrupt and startling.

In northern Belgium there were mostly houses and barns where people and animals lived, respectively, but piles of manure remained close to the buildings. We stayed at the Sheraton in Brussels for fifty-five dollars. In southern Belgium we went to a restaurant where, for twenty-nine dollars, we were served wild boar. The service was very slow. Metal slats covered the windows of many buildings.

In the city of Luxemburg we stayed at the Sheraton. In this area very few people understood English. The Sheraton was fifty-five dollars. We could have done much better but we were tired.

In the city of Luxemburg we visited the remains of a fortress that was now a park made from the ruins of what was five hundred years ago the strongest fortress castle in Europe. It was located in a sunken area of land in the center of the city. To get to this treasure of history there were tiny cobblestone streets just wide enough to let a compact car squeak through. Some of the walls had three-story houses built against their face. A natural rock was used as part of the wall openings. Small rooms two stories high had been hewn out of the rock. Small rock-walled lookout turrets contained cross-shaped openings presumably for bows and arrows. There was a set of swings in the middle of the grassy area. Terry and I walked over to the swings and sat on them. The place was very nearly deserted. There was a man there with his family. He filled us in on the history of the place. He pointed to the ruins rising many feet high on the farside of the area. Many feet above the ground and many feet from the top of the wall were cave-like openings that he explained were where warriors were stationed to defend the castle.

By the time the family left, there was only one man remaining in the park. He got out of a car and started walking toward us. I told Terry, "Don't run. Get up quietly and get in the car." By the time we got in the car, he had almost reached us. We didn't move. I suspected he was trying to figure out where we were from, as he started circling the car and looking menacingly at our Swiss plates. I was hoping the plates would not give him an answer. I was frightened but did not tell Terry. I didn't know if she was frightened. Neither of us addressed the issue. Finally, he left. I sure didn't take long leaving the area as soon as he moved away from the car.

Sidewalk cafés were popular in Belgium and Luxemburg. In Brussels the Grand Place was a large open courtyard surrounded on all four sides, where only pedestrians were allowed. Spotlights lit up the area. Two sides were lined with beautiful old buildings, while the other two sides had small shops and outside cafés lining the streets.

The population in Brussels was 95 percent Catholic. In north Belgium the people were mostly Dutch. In the south they were mostly French. There were almost no English-speaking people. They were very friendly. There was mostly countryside, with farms and small villages here and there.

We saw a cemetery for the American war dead.

Near Rotterdam, which was a seaport in southwest Netherlands, cows could be seen grazing on land in the middle of an industrial complex spewing out smoke, or they could be in a field across the street from country shops. There were canals about every two hundred to five hundred feet. Water from the canals was pumped out and used to irrigate the land, as well as used as drinking water for many animals. We stopped at a horse show. German saddles were used. Horses were of no special breed. There was not the refinement of the thoroughbreds. The lush green and flowered countryside was in sharp contrast to the drought-ridden countryside of England, where they hadn't had rain for months. In England the grass was mostly straw-colored and the earth was bare.

In Holland people were about 39 percent Catholic and 38 percent Protestant. The balance was in question. There were many thatched roofs, especially on windmills. The straw used for the roofs came from the water's edge. Much of the footwear was wooden clogs with leather uppers. All European clothing was much more subdued for women, who wore dresses everywhere. Long skirts were seen only in London. The young girls of London were just starting to wear pants. In the supermarkets, men and women used the same restrooms. Terry and I had gone into a grocery store to find something to eat. The labels on every container were written in a foreign language. It was interesting to shake things, trying to find out if there was a liquid in some of the containers and to guess what the contents might hold. In addition, no clerks understood English.

We stayed in the city of Strasbourg in northeastern France. The people of France were fairly friendly, but there was always an air of reserve. In some sections there were fewer flowers than in others. In some villages flowers were everywhere. There seemed to be very few people around. Between about noon and three, there were no people to be seen. It seemed as if we were in a foreign country for a very long time. I was happy when finally we were heading home.

Chapter 20

Thoughts on Life and Death

It was four in the morning. On June 22, 1977, I lost the school board election 606 to 626. The New York State Health Department came into the Little Flower Nursing Home and Health-Related Facility on Wednesday, the twenty-second, and again on the twenty-third, and some of them would be in on the twenty-fourth and again next Monday. I felt pummeled and unloved. Today my son John flew back to Washington to be with his girlfriend, Clare. Terry and I were alone.

Because of the time I had to spend on the Little Flower Residence and the apartments in the other two buildings—146 North Carll and 66 Park—I knew that I really didn't have the time for the school board, especially since the school district was in the middle of union negotiations. I finished the Little Flower Nursing Home union negotiations after weeks of abuse and signed a contract last Monday at nine thirty at night after an all-day session of unrest by my employees at the Kings Grant Motel in Plainview.

I felt absolutely numb. Wednesday and Thursday were filled with unending frustration. According to Miss Conrad from the health department, we should have been doing reality orientation, rehabilitation nursing, etc.

On the night of the twenty-second, I couldn't get to sleep till one in the morning. Then I was awake at four, back to sleep at seven, and then awake again at eight thirty. I had to get myself into a better frame of mind. Somehow I saw losing the election as a form of rejection by the village, and now I was being worked over by the health department. The nursing department was screwing up all over the place. There were soiled laundry bags on the floor of the soiled utility room, and meal trays going out not warm enough and not on time. The generalist concept was killing me. There was to be one inspector for everything. Because I was only the second nursing home under that concept and the health department was still learning, they all came in and did a modified version of the general inspection. *Jack, are you watching me? Do you still love me? Particularly at times like this, I miss you so much. I would give anything to have you well and here by my side. Why did you have to get sick? Where is God? Somehow today he is not my good buddy.*

Time marched on. One day blended into the next one. Hynes the special prosecutor makes hay by castigating nursing home owners. When was my turn? We were prey for all of the special interest groups who used the industry for self-gain—find a few real thieves, come in for the kill, and then pick away at the minutiae, in all nursing homes, throwing the data like pieces of meat to the devouring news media. The days of wine and roses for nursing homes were over. The industry was on the rack. The country was ripe. Unemployment was rampant. Medical care costs had been soaring, out of proportion to the cost of living, for many years. Hospitals were sacrosanct. What better scapegoat for the general ailments than the indefensible nursing home industry. After all, it was unholy and barbaric to make money on the sick and the elderly. For the hospitals with their tentacles touching all of the big deals of government and business, they would not be slandered. The hungry baying wolves, the headline-seeking media, the overtaxed, and the unemployed must all have their pound of flesh. The days would go on. The rain would fall and wash my tears away. I would drive down Southern State Parkway and watch the seasons change—the budding of spring, the full-bodied greening of summer, the changing color of fall, and the bleak browns of winter, with the glistening ice on shrubbery producing a winter wonderland or the gentle touch of snowflakes with their blanket of winter forgiveness. Initially the seasons each screamed to be heard as Jack struggled so desperately for life, but now there was only a gentle movement from one season to the other with barely a nod.

Theresa's leaving was looming toward me as a specter of death. My loneliness from Jack's death was greatly softened by her vibrant, loving presence. She would be gone, and I dreaded it so. Was I doing right by myself in not trying to keep her near me? I didn't know if it would have been selfish or just self-preserving in order to be able to function. *God, help me.* I wouldn't know until after she was gone. I didn't have John's young friends from school around anymore. A big void, or maybe even an abyss, loomed in front of me, around me, and in me.

I didn't know how I felt about Mike. I missed him dreadfully if he didn't call or I didn't see him. Was it because I needed someone, anyone, to fill a void, or did I like him a lot for him? Were we ever sure of anything? The birds were already starting their morning song. The dog Skit was a foot from my elbow, breathing heavily in a deep sleep. Motley, the German shepherd, moved in his sleep on the floor at the foot of the bed. Tomorrow would be another day.

After I'm dead, what would I have meant to my children and grandchildren? Would I have been vibrant, bright, eccentric, loving, or passionate? Would they remember I had been here and wished I still was?

I needed to write. Somehow writing was living. Words did not die. If words were used properly and frequently, and even if they were of little value currently, they would live on. Maybe that was the true link I was looking for. Could I reach back and touch my past so that I could reach forward and touch my future, not only in the form of self but in the form of descendants? Would they want to know me? I surely wanted to know them. I wanted to know Terry and John when they were sixty and seventy.

I didn't want to live forever, so why was I letting the present details of my life put me into such a tailspin? In one year from now would I wish I had this year to live over because I lived it so poorly? I didn't feel like committing suicide anymore. That must have meant something. Days and weeks and months had gone by without any of the old haunting. I did not care whether I lived or died. I was in such an awful dilemma with Jack's overwhelming and all-consuming disability. There just weren't answers to so many problems, no matter how much love, work, and concern there was.

Jack, your grave site is one of so many rows upon rows of identical small slabs of marble. You are under a rather scrawny tree. The fence bordering the cemetery is close by, with a road and mounds of funeral wreaths on the other side of the fence. I feel as though I can almost touch you as I sit here looking at your headstone, which reads, "Second World War." Damn it, should I have put you here? The high tension wires resting on their tall steel stanchions, even though they are many feet above the ground, encroach on your territory, as does the wooden fence a few yards away. Your space is so small.

Daylight was beginning to peer through the drapes. I must try to get a little more sleep.

Chapter 21

Served a Subpoena at Little Flower Nursing Home

On July 13, 1977, I was served with a subpoena from the Hynes Commission special state criminal prosecutor to appear in court the next Tuesday with all of my books and records, as noted on a twenty-four-point itemized list. Today I received a many-paged list of deficiencies from the New York State Health Department. Even the suggestions stated by the inspectors during the inspection had been added as deficiencies. I was feeling very paranoid. I had to try to keep things in the proper perspective. Each of the bureaucrats involved wanted to be somebody special. The inspectors with the highest hostility levels were the ones to flush out and record every last miserly thing that could possibly be interpreted as a deficiency. One of Jack's quotes seemed to be so appropriate, given the circumstance: "Don't let your happiness or unhappiness rest in someone else's head."

I looked around at my lovely home; I could see the water of the Carll River off in the distance. The sprinklers were arching their arms as they *putt-putt* through the different zones. The greenhouse was off at a distance. To maintain these luxuries, as well as send my children to college, I must be productive, but I did not have to take the office home. Somehow I had to do the best I could and then walk away for weekends and evenings. I had to work at not feeling a constant gnawing anxiety that was very debilitating. Anxiety dulled all pleasure, birds didn't sing, colors were flat, and sleep evaded me even when I was exhausted. Love for man and animals was turned aside or, at best, modified. Why did I let Ms. Conrad or anybody else do that to me if I could possibly avoid it? Was it possible at times to turn away from harsh surroundings? I had to avoid the abyss of anxiety.

At this point in time nothing imminent was threatening my way of life. I'd certainly, for years on end, been in much more threatening circumstances. I was not sure how or why I could get so emotionally involved with something like the health department report rather than take it as part of doing business at a nursing home and health-related facility.

Chapter 22

A Daughter Leaves Home

It was seven thirty in the evening on September 3, 1977. At approximately one thirty this afternoon I dropped Terry off at the Johns Hopkins University dorm, the Vincent, room 303. I felt as if I had one more brush with death. I was going to stay tonight, but all the kids would be at the dorms by then, and Terry needed to be with them. She already seemed to blend in, as if she had been there forever. She took her noisy little gerbil with her. Last night we secreted it into the Hilton Hotel in Pikesville, Maryland. He was so noisy we had to put him in the bathroom and close the door.

One more time night was descending and I had lost the last member of my immediate family. *My God, will I be able to withstand all of the long days and nights without her? I have loved her so!*

Chapter 23

Visiting Five Russian Hospitals, 1979

General Tourist was supposed to be superior to a travel agency. Aeroflot was the only airline in Russia. It was owned and operated by the government. Russia covered an area four times as large as the United States and comprised one-sixth of the land of the world. Its population was approximately 256 million people.

When my husband, Michael Covello, and I landed in Russia, it seemed odd to see the name Aeroflot on every plane. Almost immediately our special privileges over Russians began. We got buses first. We got served first in restaurants. As a large group of eighty-six, we were treated to the best that Russia had to offer. Of the limited food that there was, we got the best. Of the hotels that there were, we stayed at the best. Of the buses in the country, Intourist had the best fleet.

Intourist was a Russian travel agency. They handled all the movement of tourists within Russia. They furnished interpreters and buses, and arranged airport services, hotel reservations, and recreational activities.

The American tour guide was a critical person on the trip. He or she traveled with groups that had been put together to travel in Russia. We had a very superior woman who knew how to work with the interpreters furnished by in-service to guide us through mazes with cajoling, ordering, bribing, etc. She had been working for about three years for the American company that sponsored the trip.

When I was coming home on the plane, I met someone who told me about the conditions for her group of twenty-one. The group was put together by a Russian travel agency. The American tour guide was making her first trip. They moved between cities on prop planes, leaving airports one time at ten thirty, another time at midnight, and one time even later. Hotel reservations were not honored. They had to stay in a filthy hotel, with one towel for the whole floor. One woman of approximately seventy who was riding on our plane had sores about one-half inch wide going almost all the way around her mouth. She had gotten pneumonia and was taken to a Russian hospital.

Her group moved on to another city. She was left alone. After a week of being only vaguely aware of what was going on around her while getting twenty to twenty-five shots a day, food that she couldn't eat (her main sustenance was bread and eggs almost raw), she started hallucinating and demanded to be sent back to Moscow. Somehow through Intourist she managed to get back to Moscow. By accident she was placed in the same hotel as the one where her original group was housed. On the second day at the hotel, she thought she was hallucinating again. She wasn't. The group had found her wandering around the hotel lobby. When I saw her on the plane, she looked terrible. Large brown scabs covered the area around her mouth, which looked very dry. Her skin had an almost waxen look. She had traveled all over the world by herself and now had almost died in a Russian hospital. One in our group said, "She's still not out of the woods." She had two more planes to catch after landing at Kennedy before she would get to her home in Minnesota.

While touring the five Russian cities of Moscow, Tbilisi, Erevan, Baku, and Kiev, we did not see one woman driving a car, although we saw several driving trolleys. Manhattan drivers were pussycats compared to Russian drivers. On a two-lane road around hair-raising turns on a mountainside, a driver passed another vehicle while laying on the horn. Automobile drivers got pushed off roads by each other and by bus drivers. The median dividing line was used for breathtaking adventures into oncoming traffic. Would the other driver coming in our direction go off the shoulder, or were we going to crash?

The buildings between the cities were sometimes shacks that had been standing for several hundred years. The walls may be rocks held together with some form of cement or walls of logs with sheet metal roofs. Windows were frequently broken. High-rise apartments were everywhere. They were between eight and twelve stories high. Their parking lots consisted of fifteen to twenty cars. Buses were everywhere. The apartments were usually put together in large cement sections. They looked functional but poorly put together. Wherever cement work was in evidence, portions such as small corner surfaces had crumbled away. On one job site where it looked as if a trough was left partially filled with hardened cement, I stuck my fingers into the cement to feel its consistency. Much to my surprise my fingers instantly sank into very soft cement.

The red star, the hammer and sickle, and Lenin dressed in a suit and tie were everywhere. The revolution and struggling were in evidence in all of the words over buildings, signposts, billboards, and statues where the people were the children and the children's children were all children of the revolution. There were approximately 256 million Russians, of which approximately 14 million were Communists. It was an honor to be a Communist. People had to prove themselves by going through a series of test-like situations in order to be deemed worthy of joining the Communist Party. Wherever we went, all of the slogans were written in foot-high letters on the tops of buildings, on the side of the roads, on entrances to parks, etc. All proclaimed the glory of, as well as the endeavor to uphold, the revolution. There was no advertising of goods, only the extolling of struggling together for the common good. There were Lenin Squares in most, if not all of the cities we visited.

There was only one level of a four-level subway museum that did not have depictions of war or the story of a fierce struggle, the one that had been waged by Lenin up to and including the one still being waged. Military vehicles and soldiers were everywhere. Approximately one-third, sometimes more, of the vehicles on the road were military vehicles or rather small trucks, usually carrying produce or building materials. Black cars were official cars. Privately owned cars had to be a color other than black.

From two very reliable sources (one being our American guide) came the information that each of our Russian interpreters was debriefed after each trip with the Americans. I did not find out if the same was so for tourists from other countries. There were hundreds, if not thousands, of tourists concentrated mostly in Moscow and Kiev. Many were Germans, and some were from England, etc. Many others, especially in Moscow, were from Russia itself.

In all of our travels we saw only three blacks, except for a jazz group from New Orleans. There were two black students at Moscow University who were walking arm in arm with two white girls, and there was one in front of a hotel in Baku wearing a white jumpsuit imprinted with the words "Black is beautiful."

There were almost no dogs or cats in Russia. During the entire trip we saw about twenty dogs. There was one Saint Bernard, one white-haired terrier, one miniature bulldog, one Afghan, several German shepherds, and some mixed breeds.

People carried net bags in which to put their food and other purchases. Paper was of a very poor quality and used very sparingly. All of our hotels had toilet paper, with the exception of one. The paper was coarse but adequate. In all public toilet facilities, including theaters and stores, there was no toilet paper. Carrying Kleenex tissues was a must, especially since approximately halfway through the trip at least half of the group had diarrhea. It included both of us at various times. I had Lomotil with me. I was running short because of the amount I was taking and the amount I was giving away.

My husband had a sore throat that was getting worse, so we went to a Russian drugstore, thinking that maybe we could at least get cough drops. There were several counters where twenty to twenty-five items, presumably medications, were packaged in small boxes or plastic-covered sheets. The labels were all in Russian. In another counter about twenty various items, such as soap and small scissors, were shown. There was one woman in back of the medication display and another one sitting in back of a small wooden structure where there was what looked like an adding machine. We went to the medication counter, where I asked if she spoke English. No one in the store spoke English. I moved my hand up and down my throat. She showed me a medication and, without giving it to me, pointed to the woman with the machine. That woman made it known that we owed forty-six kopeck, which was the equivalent of approximately sixty-nine cents. We paid her.

She punched in numbers and then gave us a small paper receipt that came from the machine. We gave the slip to the clerk and finally got the medication. We found out from our Russian interpreter that what we were given was one of their strongest antibiotics. We then asked our Russian interpreter to write down medication for diarrhea and another for pain in the stomach. She wrote several things in Russian. We went back to the drugstore, where we showed the clerk the written request. We got medication for diarrhea, and the second medication turned out to be another antibiotic.

Old women in shabby long black garments with dark babushkas on their heads were everywhere. They were cleaning streets with short handheld brooms made of tree branches or longer brooms with the tree twigs tied to the broom handles. The more often used short brooms of about two feet long required stooping to sweep and were used in all of the cities we visited. Hotel lobbies were cleaned by cloths wrapped around the bottom of an inverted T-shaped five-foot handle with a one-foot cross piece of wood attached to the bottom. The cloth was wrapped around the bottom portion, which was pushed a few feet and then unwrapped and rinsed out in a bucket of water. This procedure was used for all mopping, as well as for the cleaning of windows in every place we visited. The old women of the country were like the worker ants of a colony. They cleaned the streets, repaired the roads using shovels, worked on scaffolds repairing buildings, waited on tables, sat behind endless desks watching every floor of the hotels, sat in hotel lobbies, dispensed room keys every time a hotel guest wanted to go to their room, and collected keys from guests leaving the hotel. In Moscow at the Rosea Hotel, which was across from the Red Square, we were handed a slip of paper to give to the desk clerk in order to get a room key. On leaving the hotel, the permission slip was given back to a guest and the room key was taken. On returning, the guest needed to produce the slip of paper to once again get their room key. One of our tour members who was romancing with another tour member did not return to her room late at night. At about midnight the woman posted on her floor was anxiously calling our Russian interpreter to ask her what to do. She was told to do nothing.

Women of Russia were not the liberated women that we saw from our vantage point here in the States. For example, medical doctors were on three levels. Most of the "more difficult jobs," such as the head of the hospital, the head of surgery, etc., were positions held by men. The government, which was the ruling class, was, as far as I could see, exclusively men. There are no visible female soldiers. Theater depicted women as dainty, colorful nymphs and men as strong, competitive he-men.

Russia was a country very much on the move. Wherever you looked, building construction was going on. It was as if Russia was only just starting to peer over the horizon of its dramatic, seemingly endless potential. The final key seemed to be missing: free enterprise. Motivation seemed to be a problem. There certainly was a difference between building a structure you would own and from which you would derive income, and building something that was owned by the state. Evidence of sloppy workmanship and practically nonexistent maintenance was everywhere. Joints didn't meet. Slabs of cement crumbled at the corners and edges but held together, as they had three times as many reinforcing rods as would be used in the States. Almost all new apartment houses resembled each other. Large cement slabs were put together with cranes. The finished product looked cheap but sturdy and functional.

In one of the hotels, I asked my husband to take a picture of slabs of cement that displayed the usual signs of poor workmanship. The stair enclosure was made of glass. I kept a lookout for the frequent raised arm accompanied by the words "Nyet, nyet" said in a loud authoritarian voice. As soon as he raised the camera, a Russian man started toward us. I whispered, "We're being watched. Let's go to the next floor. There I'll cover you a little better. Make it quick!" He raised the camera as I was turning toward the lobby stairs. The Russian floor woman had seen the move and had already started moving toward us. My husband had already gotten the picture. We hurried down the stairs looking over our shoulders.

Tourists were not allowed to photograph many areas or many of the people. This included taking pictures out of airplane windows; it also included taking pictures of army personnel, movement of army vehicles, airports, and children in training for the Communist Party. Children in training wore a red scarf around their necks. The boys wore a red star and insignia soldier patch on their shirts, while the girls wore a red scarf with an insignia on a corner of the scarf. There were many more boys among these children. We saw two or three different groups in training on the trip.

Moscow seemed devoid of children. In Moscow the average-size family had one or two children. They lived mostly on the outskirts of Russia. In the rest of the country, large families were encouraged. Abortions were discouraged but allowed. Abortions were considered shameful, as was told by one of the Russian doctors to our Russian interpreters. A woman in our group who was sitting in back of me had interpreted his words. In cities other than Moscow, some children were seen but not many. The average family had five or six children. Our hotel rooms were all very similar. The plumbing must have been made by only one company. The bathtub fixture was adjustable for hot and cold water and had a handheld showerhead on the end of a hose. Out of six bathrooms, only one had a shower curtain. Several had drains in the bathroom floor itself, as well as the regular bathtub drain. The sink, toilet, and tub were all white porcelain. The combination faucet over the sink was always the same. Out of six bathtubs and six sinks, there was only one stopper in a bathtub. In each hotel there were two four-by-one-and-a-half-foot linen towels and two very thin, coarse terry cloth towels of the same size. At least half of the time one of the plumbing fixtures was leaking. The only hotel that had a bidet as part of the bathroom fixtures was in Moscow. We had soap in all of the hotels except the one in Moscow. In three hotels it consisted of a small one-and-a-half-by-one-half-inch-thick chunk of a Fels-Naptha type of yellow soap. In one hotel we had a small chunk of pink soap that smelled like a lollipop.

The bedrooms were all very small. The two single beds were sturdy wooden-framed structures fastened to the floor and walls with a mattress, over which was placed a one-inch-thick pad and a sheet. For covers there was a woolen blanket placed through a two-foot opening of a white cotton blanket, which was covered by a spread. Pillows were two-and-a-half-foot squares, and they were four or five inches thick. They were filled with feathers. There were very poor-quality or threadbare rugs on the floor. In two of the hotels the mattress was three separate bus cushions with a cover of one-inch-thick material. They always felt as if they were separating. We stuffed towels between the cushions.

One of the women on our trip who was traveling alone had an incident in Moscow; the female Russian floor desk clerk had shoved her way into her room with her when she was returning to her room. I wanted to get all of the details, so I took a paper and a pen to her table in the dining room. In an animated fashion I wrote down the details and discussed the incident with her. She started to tell me about a second incident, where she had gotten lost in the Kremlin by herself. She was asked by two men to have her picture taken. There were plotted meetings, phone calls, etc.

All of a sudden I was aware I was being watched. A large Russian woman in the dark-blue dress of a waitress was slowly clearing a few things from farther down the table, all the while looking directly at us. She watched till I got up to leave with the rest of our group. I was halfway out of the dining room when I decided to go back for the final details. I had barely sat down before the same large woman appeared almost directly across the table from us and started picking up an unused napkin and putting it back down. I quickly changed the subject and scurried back to the hotel lobby. All of a sudden it dawned on me. She had had the incident with the floor woman, and now she had in her room a Russian newspaper with a Russian woman's name and a Russian phone number written on it by one of the men she had met under such questionable circumstances at the Kremlin.

I hurried back to the dining room to tell her I thought it would be a very good idea not to leave the newspaper in her room. By now she was seated alone in the area of the dining room where our group had been. I had barely seated myself next to her when the same Russian woman appeared, only this time she made no pretense. She stood across the table from us and stared, unsmiling, directly into our faces. The back of my neck bristled. I left immediately after a quick whispered "I wouldn't leave the paper in your room."

Some of the people on our tour were asked to take messages back to the States. The unwritten rule was not to take any messages, names, or phone numbers written by the Russian who wanted to send the message. Instead, the American was to write down the name of the US contact the Russian wanted to connect with and carry the message in his or her head.

My husband and I were walking on the streets of Erevan with another couple, looking for ice cream. It was getting dark. A young man approached us on the street. He was very anxious to get a message back to a girl who worked in the Washington area. Supposedly he was very close to having the final paperwork done on his visa so he could visit the States, so he didn't want to write her and have his visa jeopardized. We arrived at an ice cream shop, but it was closed. He offered us a ride to another ice cream place in his car. The other couple quickly refused. I turned to look toward the street. A car was at the curbside a few feet away from where we stood. A man was at the wheel. He was scrunched down and looking directly at us. He wore dark glasses even though it was dark enough to have the streetlights on. This car and driver were the transportation that we were being offered. We had been warned never to accept rides from strangers, as incidents of robbery, etc., had been reported in the past. We hurried away, hoping we weren't going to be followed, and we were grateful to get back to the hotel without an incident.

The Russian attitude toward us, as well as their conduct, varied greatly between the north and the south. Moscow's northern city was full of military and watchful and possibly vengeful eyes. We were told there were forty working churches and two synagogues in Moscow.

Almost all of the beautiful and many churches were literally intact and being preserved as museums. Some were open to the public. Churches were everywhere, all having at least several cupolas. When we questioned why crosses had been left on the tops of churches, we were told a little indignantly that was the way the churches had been and they were being preserved as they had been. One Russian guide told us that the cupolas on churches within the Kremlin were made very sheer in twelve-inch-by-twelve-inch sheets of fourteen-karat gold that had to be replaced every ten years. Another guide told us they were made of brass. Whichever metal was being used, they gleamed with a beautiful elegance in the sun.

It was so incongruous to see red stars and the hammer and sickle everywhere, and then against a blue sky the churches bore the large gold crosses on top of the gold cupolas. The Kremlin Wall, with the Red Square in front of it with its long history of bloodshed, never ceased to awe me. Here we were in a country that we had thought of as our mortal enemy. We were standing where the culmination of their very physical and psychological ideology was maintained. Where we could and could not go was very carefully watched. If a forbidden area was being transgressed by as much as several feet, a soldier raised his arm and quickly pointed to where you must move along, with quietly but firmly spoken Russian words.

When we first got to Moscow, the temperature was about 50 degrees. Two weeks later, which was our last day in the city, we were greeted by hail. The temperature was a biting, windy 40 degrees. People's breath formed a little white cloud. Heavy winter clothes were needed. The Russian people moved with a scurried intensity that did not lend itself to communication. We did not walk the streets of Moscow as we did the other cities.

We flew to Tbilisi, where the temperature was a warm 70 degrees. The actions of the people indicated curiosity. They would stare at us but usually rather unobtrusively. Many people walked the streets on Saturday. There seemed to be mostly poorly dressed people of all ages. In the hotel lobby another woman and I started to talk to some old black men who spoke English. Their ages ranged from sixty to eighty years old. They turned out to be a jazz group from New Orleans who were touring Russia under a cultural exchange program. They had been on television in the United States and were going to perform in a Russian theater nearby that night.

We didn't have tickets, so one hour before showtime we walked to the theater to see if there was any way to obtain tickets. About one hundred feet from the front door was a cluster of soldiers who stopped us. We said we were trying to get tickets. They did not understand but waved us toward the door where another cluster of soldiers stood outside of the theater entrance. They couldn't understand and finally took us to just inside, where six or seven female ushers and a couple of men were milling about. Again we asked for tickets. They didn't understand. Finally, someone said *"billet."* The word sounded reasonable, so we said yes. Someone pulled two tickets out of their pocket. The ticket said "five rubles," which was approximately $7.50. I had only American money, but my husband had seven rubles and American money. We had been warned several times to only exchange American money in places designated for such exchanges, such as hotel lobbies. We were never to use or give American money. We took a chance. We showed them that we had only seven rubles, and we took out the balance in American money. Much chattering in Russian went on. They took the money and were about to complete the transaction, when the soldiers by the door came in. There was more conversation, and then all of the money was quickly given back to us. The tickets were taken back, and almost simultaneously a woman got between the two of us and put a hand under each of our arms. She escorted us across one hundred feet of a huge darkened, empty lobby through a side door and unceremoniously led us to two of the best seats in the house. We tried giving her money to no avail. Nobody would take any money. There were ten to fifteen rows of seats in front of us and then an eight-foot-wide space for entering and leaving. There was one row of seats between us and where people entered.

When we first were ushered in, we were the sole seated occupants in a cavernous auditorium with several tiers. About twenty minutes before showtime, several couples sat directly in front of us. Four girls sat to my left. I asked if they spoke English. The answer was no, but the one I asked stood and waved and called to a friend halfway across the auditorium. She came and sat by me. She was an eighteen-year-old girl studying to be a podiatrist. In back of me was an eleven-year-old boy who understood some English. He was there with his mother and his teacher. After talking for some time and feeling a great deal of warmth emanating from them, I asked if they would like to correspond. They both answered yes with a great deal of enthusiasm. Not knowing whether they might get in trouble if they gave me their addresses, I gave each of them a business card. There was more conversation. The boy's mother had him give me a pair of opera glasses. She and his teacher, even though they couldn't speak English, were positively beaming. The girls were bubbly, giggly, and pleasant with sweet open faces, and they chattered endlessly among themselves in Russian.

Seated in the row in front of us were two city officials who had many men greet them with a kiss on the check, a smile, and pleasantly spoken Russian words. The people in the theater probably represented the upper middle class. They had a completely different appearance than the people we had seen on the street. The chatting, giggling teenagers, except for their language and the clothes they wore, could have been from anywhere in the States. Jeans were everywhere. One-quarter to one-third of the young people and a few of the adults wore them. On close scrutiny, other fabrics presented a nice appearance but were far below the quality and workmanship of American clothes.

It was considered very impolite to leave the theater during a performance. Almost all of the seats were filled. After about an hour the audience started to stir a little. A few brave souls left early, including our eighteen-year-old new acquaintance. Before she left, she volunteered her name and address, which I immediately took, so I felt it was okay for me to ask the boy in back of us for his name and address. Without any hesitation he gave it to me, along with his birthday. We were the center of much attention, most of which was openly friendly, but there were some people being rather guarded. When the jazz leader at the end of a few selections made the sign of the cross, I caught a look of anger pass between the village official and his wife seated in front of us.

We traveled by bus from Tbilisi to Erevan, where the temperature was in the eighties. As in other Russian cities, Lenin was very much in evidence and always portrayed in a business suit and tie. In the hotter climates of Russian cities, the people were darker-skinned, dark-eyed, and poorly dressed. Many of the young men traveled in groups of three or more. The approaches by men were open and sometimes frightening. At dusk, waiting in Lenin Square for waterworks that never took place, Americans seemed almost like prey. Four or five women from our group sat on the opposite side from my husband, me, and another couple. The women were quickly surrounded by a milling, loudly talking group of fifteen or twenty young, swarthy-looking Armenian men. Finally, an older woman disengaged herself from the group and came over to us. She said they had just been told by a young man who spoke English to disband and not talk anymore. He had now moved to the back of our group and was anxiously looking over to the other side. Man after man would closely and boldly scrutinize me from top to bottom. A woman's purse was snatched, but only one strap broke and she managed to hang on.

One of our Russian guides and one of our American guides went walking with one American man from our group. Young men were openly making passes. The Russian girl told the American man to put one of his arms around each of them. It made no difference. The Russian Armenians determined that the two English-speaking people were together and our Russian tour guide was the extra. They ran their fingers over her arms while suggesting she go off with them. They managed to get away and get back to the hotel without further incidents.

Next our group took a flight to Baku, a city overlooking the Aspen Sea. On a boat ride we passed an area where we were warned not to take pictures. Off in the distance we saw Russian Navy ships. We saw oil drilling everywhere—coming into the city, standing in the sea, and leaving the city. Many had rusted machinery with nothing moving. On the outskirts of the city, the industrial stench was similar to New Jersey's industrial areas and hung thick and nauseating in the air. The wells moved slowly in a rhythmic motion like that of a duck's bill moving toward the ground and up again.

This city was so warm that nights were very uncomfortable and we were perspiring despite using no bedcovers. Mosquitoes made this our first and last experience with any bugs other than flies. Our hotel room overlooked Lenin Square. Several nights at ten thirty we saw three groups of navy men smartly marching down the street. When walking down the street with my husband, we were stared at endlessly. I began to feel as if I wore two heads. The men were rather bold in their looking but not to the extent of Erevan.

When we asked to get a picture of a telephone repairman and his helper, by pointing at our camera and then him, he quickly agreed. The tools he was using would have been primitive for an American household toolbox. We had no more than taken the picture when an angry thirty-five-year-old woman came along who seemed to berate the workman in no uncertain terms for letting us take his picture. Later when we tried to get a picture of the first male street cleaner that we had seen, as he started to pose, a large imposing Russian woman of about sixty stepped between us. She angrily spoke to him and would not leave. We hung around for a few minutes but then were afraid to get him in trouble, so even as we slowly made our way to the corner and kept looking back, she never left him. An hour later we went back to peer around the corner. She was still there.

My husband had had his shoes shined. We needed to have one of our shoes repaired, so we went back to the man who had shined his shoes. I was ceremoniously and with a great deal of deference given a chair he placed outside of his small shanty located on the side of a building. My husband was given a chair inside. While he was repairing the shoe and after we had managed to communicate to the number of children among all of us, I pointed to our ever-present camera. He smilingly said, "Nyet." We could get what seemed to be a more natural response from people when we hid our camera, which we did in my handbag.

On our personal street tour of this city, we came upon a marble monument. A flame was burning in front of a huge marble head. Wreaths had just been placed in front of the monument. Five or six people were having what seemed like professional pictures taken. Among them was a person who looked like a Russian dignitary. He had buttons of all sorts literally covering his chest. I told my husband I would love to have my picture taken with him, but it probably would be considered extremely gauche. He went and asked. Not only did he pose for us, but I was asked by their hand motions to pose with the military man for his photographer, who took two different shots. Then my husband was asked to pose for one shot with the military man. I think they wanted our names after that, but we didn't volunteer. They had enough already for Russian propaganda. I was a little concerned about how the pictures taken by the Russian photographer might be used.

Down the street was a place where fish had just been delivered. There was a long line of people waiting to purchase the fish that were being unpacked from wooden barrels. The fish were placed into the people's net shopping bags, from which heads and tails were protruding, or a half dozen fish would be slapped on paper that was folded over the fish. A man dropped his fish purchase on the sidewalk. He quickly bent down, slapped the fish back into the paper, and walked off.

From the city we went to a rug-weaving factory. Five girls sat in front of each loom. Their ages appeared to range from about fourteen to thirty. Intricate colorful patterns evolved from flying fingers threading and knotting each and every yarn that made up the average size of six feet by eight feet and took four months to make. The rugs sold for about three thousand dollars. The patterns had been memorized by most of these dark-skinned, dark-eyed girls. Their expressions ranged from fear to happiness, with repeated phrases like "What is your name?" Their dresses were made of very cheap cotton, and many had kicked off their sandals. Flies were frequently seen resting undisturbed on bare legs and arms. The girls worked forty-hour weeks with one hour off for lunch. Their pay was 100 to 150 rubles ($150 to $225) a month. Our American travel guide in training quizzed the Russian interpreter with "You don't give them coffee breaks in the morning and afternoon?" I told her she sounded like a union organizer. A conference room was decorated with pictures of special rugs that had been woven. A very special rug with Lenin's picture in the middle was hung in a Russian museum. Propaganda literature lay around the room.

We flew to our next tour destination of Kiev. It was an old city of parks with many flowers and many tourists. If given only a cursory look, the city could be taken for any metropolitan area in the United States. People were fair-skinned. Blond hair and blue eyes were not oddities. Stores were stocked with more goods. People were better dressed even though we were still looked at but now unobtrusively again. The weather was about fifty degrees and chilly.

Additional Notes on the 1979 Russian Hospital Study Tour

Russian hospitals were roughly thirty to forty years behind American hospitals in all aspects, from the infrastructure to medical equipment. The hospitals we visited had been informed of our scheduled visit one year before the fact.

Moscow

Everybody was attached to a district outpatient clinic. A patient could go to a clinic or call a doctor to go to their home and be seen in twenty minutes.

Medical doctors at the clinics were there from eight in the morning to eleven at night. The numbers 03 were dialed for an ambulance. Ambulances usually had one medical doctor, two nurses, and one junior medical assistant. The clinics were staffed with 80 percent female doctors. Surgeons were men. The more difficult jobs were given to men. Hospitals were staffed with 40 percent male doctors.

The clinic building was five stories high and approximately two hundred feet long. It was a sixty- to seventy-year-old building with porcelain tubs and sinks as old as the building.

Therapeutic treatments included X-ray therapy; hydrostatic therapy (powerful water jets, as from hoses used on fire trucks), used for obesity; mud therapy or mud tampons; acupuncture; medicines; and water inhalation (for ear, nose, and throat infections).

Lenin's picture was in every room.

Tbilisi

The hospital was nine years old and contained one thousand beds. There were 259 doctors, 450 nurses, and 450 nurse's aides associated with the hospital.

Baku

At the veterans hospital, the patients got very special treatment. A woman traveling with us broke a leg. Wheelchairs and crutches seemed impossible to get.

Russia

Eighty-six people traveled to Russia on a hospital study tour in 1979. The group was divided into three for busing and for American and Russian tour guides.

There were ninety-two medical schools in Russia, out of which 28,000 medical doctors graduated each year. The country had 880,000 medical doctors. Russia had one-third of the doctors in the world, with 70 percent of them being women. Students currently being admitted to medical school were 50 percent boys and 50 percent girls. It was very difficult to get into medical school. Only one out of seven or eight were accepted. There were three categories of doctors and nurses. Every year exams were given; if the students passed, they could go from one level to the next. Salaries depended on the different levels, their work records, and quotas reached during which they got 60 to 100 percent of the maximum salary. After six years, they got 100 percent.

The first level was the candidate of science. The second level was the doctor of science. And the third level was the doctor of academia. In order to become a medical doctor, one must have secondary education plus six years of training, one year in a hospital, and three years in an assigned area. Good grades meant receiving grants to go to school. Eighty-five percent of students received grants.

Registered nurses studied for ten years at a secondary level and then two and a half years at a higher level.

Pregnant women received four months of paid leave and could stay out a year.

The description of special homes for the aged resembled that of places in the United States that would fall between the care given in adult homes and nursing homes. They had mental hospitals.

Life expectancy was seventy to seventy-five years, with about two extra years for women.

The state had the only health system, and it was free. Medicine was very inexpensive. Doctors and nurses were sent for training every five years. They went to Moscow for six months at the Central Institute for Advanced Knowledge.

The most prevalent categories of conditions were cardiovascular, cancer, and trauma.

Clinic or ambulance people decided whether someone should be admitted to a hospital.

The people traveling in our study group were introduced as "comrades" in a hospital.

Hospitals had metal bed frames holding up thin mattresses. There were no call systems except in intensive care. A 565-bed hospital had six beds for intensive care.

Hospitals had primitive-looking labs. American high schools had more sophisticated labs.

Abortions were allowed, but it was a shameful thing to talk about. Propaganda encouraged having many children. Circumcision was allowed only if medically indicated.

Hospital stays were seven to nine days for childbirth and two days for a tonsillectomy.

Moscow

On September 20, 1979, a truckload of soldiers drove past. There were trucks and military vehicles everywhere. It appeared as if one-third of people and vehicles were military.

Screens on apartment houses consisted of cheesecloth. Most had no screens. Curtains were sparse white cotton and covered only the lower portion of the windows.

People lined up to buy three pumpkins. A second line was to buy cabbage.

The Kremlin was completely surrounded by a forty-foot wall. The czar walled himself in. The wall was five to fifteen meters high and three to sixteen meters thick. It had twenty towers. Five towers were topped with red stars made of ruby glass. Red meant "beautiful." Kremlin meant "fortress." Nobody lived there. There were some crosses in place to preserve things as they once were. The Assumption Cathedral was built in 1479. Cathedrals were state museums. The Kremlin was the seat of the government. The secretary was inside. Communist headquarters were outside. Of the 1,500 members of parliament, more than 435 were women. Within Kremlin Walls were gold-covered cupolas on some roofs. The cupolas were shaped like an upside-down turnip, with some bearing crosses. I saw a red star on one in the background. The gold leaf on the domes was replaced about every ten years.

There were department stores for children.

A slogan on a billboard with a picture of people marching stated, "All power in society belongs to the people. We would like to turn Moscow into a model city." There were almost no window displays in store windows.

There were many references to prerevolutionary and postrevolutionary life. For example, one building was used prerevolutionary and the probability was that it was now a museum. Churches were preserved for viewing. All churches were nonfunctioning. There were two Catholic churches, two synagogues, and fifty-five Russian Orthodox churches. Few people lived in the center of the cities, so there were very few children seen on city streets. Most people rented from the state, and rents comprised 4 to 5 percent of the average budget. Sometimes people waited two or three years to be able to get a rental. They could own if they could pay 40 percent on a sale and pay off the balance over fifteen years. On average, five hundred apartments were being built every day. We were housed in the Rossia Hotel, across the street from the Red Square. All passports were confiscated at the front desk and doled out again upon leaving the hotel. There was no heat in the hotel. The temperature outside was about 40 or 50 degrees. If lights were used at all, they were used very sparingly.

The US Embassy was a fairly modest two-and-a-half-story structure. Russia did not have a service-oriented culture. There were very few cabs.

There was no unemployment. They needed more people to work.

Russia was getting ready for the Olympics. Several hundred soldiers stood in formation. Soldiers were everywhere.

My husband asked, "Can I take a picture with my wife?" The solder shook his head no.

The arena held 106,000 people. There were 30,000 students at Moscow University and 6,000 postgraduate students. Children studied for ten years, finishing at seventeen years old, at which time they could enter higher education. There were fifty-three universities in the country. There were many more applicants for the humanities—literature, languages, etc.—than for technical, such as engineering. The rent for dorms was three rubles per month. The more a student studied, the more he or she earned. The average salary was 160 rubles a month. Students could get from twenty to five hundred rubles for a forty-hour workweek, with Saturday and Sunday off. Schoolchildren from first to eighth grade went to school six days a week from nine o'clock to noon or one. Ninth and tenth graders attended school from nine o'clock to three o'clock. All students had to work for three years after they graduated. If someone wanted to own a home, they couldn't own one in Moscow; it had to be outside the city limits. In Moscow, people could own an apartment. Taxes were 13 percent of salaries.

An ugly American asked a Russian, "Wouldn't you work harder if you could get more money?"

Medical services were free of charge. Everybody was attached to a district outpatient clinic, called a polyclinic, where 60 to 100 percent of the medical doctor's salary was paid. After six years they got 100 percent. Almost everybody got an annual medical checkup. Preventive medicine was stressed. Pregnant women were given a paid four-month leave. They were allowed to take a one-year leave. There were 92 medical schools training 28,000 medical doctors a year. There were 880,000 medical doctors in the country. They had one-third of the medical doctors in the world, of which 70 percent were women. Now students were 50 percent boys and 50 percent girls. There were forty thousand people associated with this clinic. There was a medical doctor for every section. All specialists worked here. They went to the home if necessary. Patients could call a doctor to go to their home or they could be seen at the clinic. Patients could call an ambulance and, in thirty minutes, get first aid. The first thrust was prevention. Doctors watched people with chronic diseases. They came every three to six months to the clinic for observation. The patients' cards were in their files. The hospital had one thousand beds. When patients were discharged, their charts were sent to the clinic, where the patient was followed. The clinic had a staff of 220 people, 80 doctors, and 95 nurses, with the rest of the staff servicing the building.

Every five years for six months, doctors and nurses went to the Moscow Central Institute for Advanced Knowledge to learn the newest methods and treatments. Salaries for doctors and nurses depended on their work record, which had three categories. Every year that they passed exams, they could go from one level to another. Medical doctors worked here at the clinic and at the hospital. There was a medical doctor here from eight in the morning till eleven at night. If an ambulance was called several times during the night, then a medical doctor was called and in the morning he saw the patient. The ambulances were centralized. Most districts had ambulances. People dialed 03 for an ambulance. Usually the person calling was asked why he or she was calling. Specialists would go to the house. If the situation was serious, the person was taken to the hospital. Usually there was one medical doctor, two nurses, and one junior medical assistant. In this clinic 80 percent were women. Surgeons were men, as the job was more difficult. In the hospital, 40 percent were men. People could pay to go to an outpatient clinic. The money went to the state.

All patients were seen in the X-ray room once a year. Doctors treated borderline mental patients in a special psychiatric clinic, and there were mental hospitals. Clinic or ambulance personnel decided whether someone should be admitted to the hospital.

Pills and injections were available for birth control. Abortions were allowed. Women could decide whether to have an abortion. Propaganda promoted having more children. There weren't many teenage abortions. There were no cases of child abuse. The elderly and senile were seen in their homes. Drugstores delivered medications to them. There was a network of homes for the elderly. If they got lonely or had problems, they could go to the homes.

Visiting nurses managed chronic diseases in people's homes. If people were sick enough, they went to hospitals. There was no day care. Few old people lived alone. Traditionally they lived with their families. Families could send the elderly to homes for the aged for short periods of time. The homes usually had four stories and accommodated four hundred people. Patients had a room of their own with their own furniture. They had their own outpatient clinic. There was a special home for elderly actors. Sometimes homes were divided according to a disease. There were hospitals for the disabled who came mostly because of wartime injuries. It took fifteen to thirty minutes to answer a call. They tried to keep patients alive, even if it was for an extra day. Life expectancy was from seventy to seventy-five years of age.

Doctors were trained in medical schools. There would be secondary education of six years and then one year in the hospital. High schools were secondary, and then at seventeen years old students went on to medical school for seven more years. Medical school entrance exams were very hard to pass. There were seven to eight people for every place in medical school.

After secondary school, nurses went on for three more years of training. They worked five-day weeks, six-and-a-half-hour days. There were some courses for aides. Their record of work determined their level of one, two, or three. Every five years they had to take a test. Parents usually decided which specialty schools children went to. After eighth grade, children could go to a vocational training center. After graduating, they had to work at appointed places for three years. They could go any place in the SSR after three years. Students in the education process were paid grants, which included 85 percent of the students if they got good grades.

Helicopters and planes, not trains, were used to bring care to outlying districts.

The state health system was the only one. The state owned everything.

Kiev District, # 102, Moscow, Dr. Zvetkova, Chief Doctor

The clinic building was a sixty- to seventy-year-old five-story building of approximately two hundred feet long. It was very clean but not in good repair. There was a lot of tile used on walls. The porcelain tubs and sinks were as old as the building. There were different areas for X-ray therapy and hydrostatic therapy. There was mud therapy, including mud tampons; acupuncture; an analysis laboratory; and ear, nose, and throat therapy, including medication and water inhalation. The treatment room had about twenty cubicles with water hoses that looked like the size of those on fire trucks that shoot water at the patients from a distance.

The walls were all painted white, with rooms starkly furnished and decorated. Lenin's picture was in every room. Some plants and floral arrangements were in the waiting rooms.

People usually responded to smiles.

Old stooped women swept the streets with a stick, which had a small bundle of tree branches tied on one end.

Property was owned either personally or by the state. Personal property in Russia was the same as anywhere else in the world. It was sacred.

There were 120 miles of subways. The subway elevators were approximately one hundred feet long. People on the escalator who didn't want to keep walking stood single file on the right. The walkers walked quickly down the left side of the moving stairs.

Revolution was depicted in every statue, painted sign, and mosaic in the subway. The subway was more like a museum than a subway, with bronze statues, paintings, and marble floors and walls. In the waiting area, there were lovely wooden benches and crystal and chrome chandeliers.

Before the revolution, 80 percent of the people were illiterate. Now twenty years later, the literacy rate was 100 percent. It took us only two or three months to build a building. The rent that is charged today was the same as it was in 1929.

Each district had a palace of marriage. The procedure is to go for one month before registration of which at least two weeks are given to meditation. The couple and two witnesses went by special arrangement at a certain time to the marriage palace. The couple exchanged rings and then listened to a speech about their future life and duties. The small party went to a neighboring room after the ceremony and then the wedding. The following celebration took place in a restaurant or similar place. Most of the weddings took place on Friday or Saturday and were celebrated on Sunday. People could have Christian marriages. Prior to such a marriage, the couple must go for registration. A Christian marriage was not recognized by the state. If a divorce happened, the father would not have to pay alimony. If a couple was not married but lived together and had children and then became separated, the woman could go to court to get alimony for the children. Children were considered adults once they turned eighteen. At that point they could marry and work.

The rate of divorce was very high and second only to the United States. There was one divorce for every three marriages, except for Moscow, which had one divorce for every two marriages. If the married couple had no children and there were no objections, the divorce proceedings were easy. They registered at certain times of the day, filled out forms, and paid money. It was simple. If one person was against the divorce, they went to a court hearing. The first of two courts was for reconciliation, where the couple had two or three months to make up. If the first court did not work, the second court would issue a divorce. In a divorce, the ex-husband paid 25 percent of his salary for a child. There was no alimony if both partners worked. If the woman was able to work, the man didn't have to pay. A medical commission decided if a wife couldn't work. When there were two children, the man paid 33 percent of his salary. If there were three or more children, the man paid 50 percent of his salary. If the division of property was decided between the couple, it was okay when they went to court.

When people reached retirement age, they received 70 percent of their yearly salary.

At the hotel a young lady gave me various details of her experiences. After she received a key to her room, she was followed down the hall by one of the hotel employees. When she turned the key in the door, she was shoved into the room. They were making stroking motions, indicating they wanted to buy her clothes, an umbrella, shoes, and a leather coat, and this went on for at least thirty minutes. They really wanted her fancy shoes at the Rosea in Moscow. Another time she was asked for gum, a waiter even asked for her corduroy jeans.

One of the young female tourists on our trip who didn't seem ready to follow the rules got lost at the Kremlin in the middle of a large group of Russians. Two well-dressed men came over to her. One said he was from Poland, while the other one said he was from Moscow. They said they wanted to take a picture with her. They took a picture and then asked for her name and address. She gave it to them. They told her that if she came back to the same place at nine o'clock the next morning they would be there to give her the picture. She said no, that she was leaving at six in the morning. They told her that they had a daughter who spoke English. They gave her the daughter's name and phone number and then gave her very specific instructions. She was to call the daughter at eight in the morning on the first of the month. They told her, "Don't call from the hotel. Go downtown to call. If you call, don't tell her what you want. She will bring the picture to you. Just mention the time you can meet her." They walked her back to the hotel. We were told it was a common occurrence for Russians to try to get messages back to people in the States.

Buses went in and out among miles of apartment housing projects outside Moscow. On September 22, 1979, after approximately fifteen miles we had seen no private homes. Apartment buildings ranged from sixteen to twenty-two stories high. The construction of apartment houses was going on everywhere. Twenty-five miles outside of Moscow was nothing but open fields. Older buildings were not in very good repair. I wondered whether it was because they all belonged to the state and were not privately owned. Next to the road was a large greenhouse that had obviously been abandoned. Women were seen carrying buckets over their shoulders. The forests that we drove past were mostly made up of pine and white birch trees. There were no trees with large trunks that would indicate an old stand of trees. On the way to the airport, first came apartments and then fields, followed by a few more apartment houses, and then the airport came into view. Fifty churches had their doors open in Moscow. All of the churches had a number of cupolas. Monasteries also served as fortresses.

Farmers sold produce at flea markets. There were about ten in Moscow. The one we saw was in a large building. The vegetables were very small in size and very limited in quantity compared to what was available in our US markets. There were a couple of unbelievably scrawny plucked chickens hanging by their feet. The parking lot held about ten to fifteen cars. Eight-story apartment buildings had approximately ten to fifteen cars in their parking lots. Buses leaving apartment houses were packed with many people standing from the front all the way to the back.

Of our three different Russian interpreters, one seemed rigidly party line, one in between, and the third one not very much.

At a circus ten flags were hanging that represented ten different countries. Among them were Yugoslavia, Cuba, Romania, Latvia, Bohemia, and Russia. There were slides of political figures shown along with the circus acts. The first act was an aerialist with two girls jumping off swings. There were trained horses, as well as trained cats and dogs, doing a number of different tricks.

On September 25, 1979, we arrived at Hotel Ani in Erevan, which was an Armenian republic.

There were regular funerals. Cremation was allowed. If asked for, ashes would be buried in a cemetery. Conversation the night before with Russian interpreters and our tour guides touched on Russians going to the country. We overheard the word "Venezuela." It turned out that was where Russian business managers established citizenship and infiltrated by establishing cells of Communist sympathizers.

In Tbilisi, Georgia, there was a Russian speaker at the General Hospital who was the first assistant of the chief doctor. The candidate of science was a doctor in the Armenian republic. He was a nephropathologist. It was one of the largest hospitals and had three departments. The first was a hospital with one thousand beds. The second was the emergency department that dealt with different suburban districts and the Erevan clinic. It was called a republic because different districts were associated with it. The third was the Methodical Organization Department, where seminars were held for the doctors from the clinics who were sent here to learn. They served as consultant clinics for cardiology, neurology, endolymphatic, resuscitation, artificial breathing, and intensive care. All eighteen departments had specialties. They were ranked first among hospitals and had been awarded a red banner three times for their good work. The hospital was built in 1970.

The Medical Institute had a permanent school with eight chairs and twelve professors. There were 259 doctors. One of them was a doctor of medical science, which was academia's highest degree. There were three levels: a candidate of science, a doctor of science, and a doctor of medical science. There were 450 nurses who worked in the hospital and about 450 nurse's aides. The average length for surgical procedures was eighteen to twenty days. For a kidney nephrology procedure, the average stay was thirty days. The orthopedic department dealt with rehabilitation. Attached to this hospital but away from the general hospital, people were taught to walk, etc.

On September 26, 1979, a male doctor came to speak to us. He assisted the chief surgeon.

There was only one nursing home in the whole district, and the number of people living there was very small. There were eight nurses and four nurse's aides.

Patient records were kept for thirty years.

A table had been set up for us once we got back to the conference room, with the doctors and nurses bringing in their own foodstuffs.

Baku

On September 27, 1979, we stayed at Hotel Azerbaijan. This city and the last one we visited had some of the same characteristics. The young men were more forward in their approach to tourists. It was very warm, 80 degrees or more. The people, especially the young men, openly stared at us at night and sometimes during the day. We found young men following in step next to us or behind us. In Erevan at eight o'clock at night one of our Russian guides and a man from our tourist group were walking in Lenin Square. Several young men started following them and wouldn't leave them alone.

In Baku my husband and I and another couple went walking, looking for a place to buy ice cream. We were approached by a young man who was coaxing us to get in his car so he could help us to get ice cream. He finally gave the woman with us the name and place of a girl he knew in the Washington area. He wanted to get in touch with her and give her a message.

Lenin was everywhere. He and sometimes Baryshnikov stared from billboards, statues, and signs.

The head of the hospital in Baku, Dr. Asivick Comel, greeted us at the door. This district, Narimanov, had one general hospital. There were ten administrative districts with a political leader and a doctor. The industrial district had many departments in the hospital: surgery, neurology, cardiology, pulmonary, gastroenterology, and many others. The doctor introduced the nurse as comrade chief nurse. Each department had a senior nurse. The main task of the doctors and nurses was to help the patients to recover. First, the patients came to the hospital reception area, where the treatment was free. The building was ten years old and had 565 beds. There was a hospital for children with TB. There were four general hospitals. There were special houses for old people. There are about 70 medical doctors and 231 nurses. In the city, schools had special courses for nurses. Medical doctors had two shifts of six and a half hours, while nurses had eight-hour shifts.

The stay in the hospital for childbirth was seven to nine days. The stay for a tonsillectomy was two days. There were six beds in intensive care, with an average stay of five days.

Kiev

The city was founded in the tenth century. There were many tourists in this city. A department store had hundreds of people waiting outside for it to open.

A Russian Orthodox church had people active in and around it at ten o'clock on a Sunday morning. Inside were many older women with kerchiefs over their heads. They lined the inner walls, with some disabled and in contraptions to transport them. A few had crutches. Several seemed blind. The church had no pews. It was packed with people milling about. Old women with their babushka-covered heads seemed to be everywhere. Mostly these were working-class people. Many people were kissing holy pictures that had been placed in glass. A towel hung over a metal bar was used to wipe the glass before it was kissed.

Just inside the front door, old women sat in back of tables selling different-sized candles. I bought a small candle. After locating Jesus on a cross, I had difficulty trying to light the candle, as the setup was not similar to our US churches. An old woman held my hand, showing me how. In the middle section of the church, a sermon was being preached. People were jammed together around the preacher. They were packed almost two-thirds of the way back from the front of the church. Strong body odors clung in the air. Candle stands that were bought at the entrance were next to each of the elaborately covered pictures.

Sitting in one corner was an old female beggar. She was partially covered with rags and had very small bundles on the floor around her. Her black clothes were terribly shabby, and she wore a black kerchief. Her hands appeared dirty and puffy. She seemed blind. Her body was bent forward. I walked several steps toward her and reached down to give her several coins. Before I touched her, her hand quickly turned palm up. She took the coins and made the sign of the cross and kissed it. She slipped them into one of her many bags. In one of her bags I could see several apples.

Out by the gate at the street stood six or seven male and female beggars. They all looked like the US version of the Bowery bums. One had hideously grotesque deformities. One arm was missing above the elbow. The other arm stopped several inches from what would have been a wrist. The church was in an area with many tourists, so my husband and I left our group and took off on our own. In a courtyard in back of the church of Saint Basil's, we sat on a park bench. In the courtyard sat a grandmother and a child of about three. After I looked at the child with a friendly smile, she came over to give me a chestnut. She then started coming over with leaves. I finally had about twelve leaves. With every leaf that she gave me, my husband and her grandmother laughed heartily. She would then run back to her grandmother to get another leaf for me. When we got up to go, she quickly came back to collect her treasures. The language barrier was once again overcome. We all laughed together and threw each other kisses as we left.

We went out for a walk and stopped in front of a store window. Soon we started talking to two young men. The one we could understand had not spoken English for ten years but made himself understood. The two were Russian cadets in training to be flyers. They worked in a scientific laboratory exploring infrared ground-to-air heat-seeking missiles guided by infrared rays.

He told us the salespeople in Russia had sales quotas to meet. The first three Sundays of the month they had to close. If by the last Sunday of the month they had not made their quota, they had to remain open.

General Information on Visiting Five Russian Hospitals

Intourist provided three buses, two Russian tour guides who traveled with us, and three Russian interpreters. In each city that we visited, there might be a tour of the city in the morning or a visit to a hospital or clinic at one or two in the afternoon and tours to various points of interest. On some occasions, the evening affair consisted of a welcome dinner that included not only the food but wine, beer, champagne, and vodka. Local music was played. Other evenings included a circus, a folk festival, etc. The day's activities and mealtimes were posted in the lobby of the hotel. Two Russian tour guide interpreters made the entire trip with us. They helped our American tour guide navigate through airports, make hotel accommodations, and get through a myriad of problems, such as getting an extra towel or being advised about a local custom to follow. It was considered very rude to take a coat into the seating area of a restaurant or theater. Well-manned coat-hanging areas were everywhere, and we were expected to use them even when we were freezing.

Moscow didn't turn on the heat in buildings until October 15. The most heat we had anywhere was from a one-inch pipe in the bathroom. Through this pipe hot water ran, so we only felt a little bit of heat in the bedroom if the bathroom door was left open.

We had a range of Russian tour guides. Some had snippy party-line attitudes, and then there was the always smiling, calm, good-natured Tanya. No matter how good-natured a Russian guide was, one of their most often repeated phrases was a bit impatient "Of course" in response to many of the questions that we asked. One of our guide's family was divided between being Communists and non-Communist. She informed us that a divided family was very common in this country of 14 million Communists among its 256 million people.

Erevan had a large fair-like exhibit of the country's accomplishments spread out over hundreds of acres. Buildings dotted the land here and there. Transportation was provided in little electric open cars. The first car pulled three or four cars in back of it. People were seated facing each other. We had an additional Russian guide for this little trip. An example we were given for what was going on in the various buildings was cattle breeding. We were not allowed to stop at any building except one, which had demonstrations of outer space travel. Around the buildings where animals were supposedly being cared for, there were no signs of bucolic life or people. There were no small piles of manure and no animal smells. The building and grounds seemed to be getting only marginal upkeep.

Our guide was anything but friendly. Going through the space center, I asked her how long a particular vehicle had been in space. "Long enough" was the curt answer. She didn't let up. The tour through the building was rushed. At each exhibit the explanation concerning the exhibit was given us from a recording. We walked from there to the entrance to the grounds. Only one other building had people coming and going through the doors. When asked about the space center, our guide never missed a step, heading us straight for the entrance as she answered in three words something that sounded like opportunities we had through BOCES in the United States. At the door our Russian guide took off.

About eight of us were left milling around the outside entrance. Three busloads of soldiers drove up and started pouring into the entrance area. Red stars on soldiers' hats were always in evidence, but I was always curious as to where they were from. Skittishly we drew a little closer. Someone asked the soldiers if anyone spoke English. One did. He came over several feet from his comrades and started speaking Hungarian to one of our group. He was from Hungary. He almost immediately was told to stop talking to us. He stopped and moved back several feet to once again become indistinguishable from the other soldiers.

In all of the cities we visited, there were special stores where only tourists could shop. The Russian people were not allowed inside. Here there was a better variety of goods than in a similar display of like products in the stores for the general population. The prices charged in the tourist stores were approximately three-quarters or two-thirds of those for exactly the same goods available to the Russians in their stores. We looked into many stores. Clothes were one and a half times as expensive as in American stores. In addition, the quality of the fabric and the workmanship were far inferior. The selection of goods was very limited and of a poor quality. People lined up everywhere in the streets in front of stands, which had a selection of canned fish, canned tomatoes, fresh fish, onions, apples (all green-skinned and small), grapes (purple and green), pomegranates, etc.

Masses of people were in front of the department stores before they opened. Inside one store we found a large pile of black rubber boots, with as many as twenty-five or more people all shoving and shouting. Some had gotten one boot from the pile and now were trying to get to the counter to get the matching second boot. We stood to one side observing, only to find several people in another spot observing us. Grocery stores were everywhere. Usually the setup was very similar. There would be three sections each with about fifteen to twenty selections. One section would have open ten-pound bags of cornmeal, wheat, flour etc. One open bag held seasonings. Another section had a meat counter, which would be either refrigerated or on a table with flies buzzing around. The floor area covered about three feet by four feet. It was impossible to distinguish what animal the meat came from or what cut of meat it was. What there was had about two-thirds fat, with the lean portion never grained with fat. The meat could be a piece six inches across with two inches of lean meat in the middle or long strips similar in shape to a sausage or any shape in between. Cheeses of different kinds were in greater quantities. Milk came in about two-cup glass containers. Milk was never served in restaurants. We didn't venture to buy milk in the stores, because we didn't know if it was pasteurized. Buttermilk was sometimes served in restaurants. Canned and smoked fish were frequently used. The third area of the grocery stores held fifteen to twenty selections of canned fruit and vegetables. Some stores sold bread and/or baked goods. Bread was unwrapped. Sometimes people carried it under their arm or in a net bag or in their hands. We saw small melons and some apples being carried in net bags on planes. The Russian people spent much time and effort waiting in endless lines shopping for food. Buying food in small quantities seemed to be done daily.

The meals served to us included at various times cheese and then more cheese, sausage (which was two-thirds fat in large chunks), smoked salmon, caviar, sardines, fried potatoes, rice, a form of vegetable soup, canned peas, white and/or brown bread, and butter. Tea, coffee, beer, mineral water, and ice water were available at most meals. The beef served was usually in small quite tough pieces except for two times where the piece was fairly large and tender. In addition, we were sometimes served sliced tomatoes with onions, a fig jam, and eggs. Dessert usually consisted of a quite good vanilla ice cream with a spoonful of preserves. Infrequently there was a small, very thin piece of a heavy cake or a cookie. There was never a pie or a pudding or light fluffy cakes. Grapes were frequently served, and several times dessert was a peach.

Bookstores were very interesting. There might be as many as one hundred books to sell. The few pictures on the covers of books were of Lenin or the military. Most of the books had dark, drab, one-color covers with very little writing. There were no magazines and only one Russian newspaper of a few pages.

Here and there were small shops that sold handbags or shoes or both. The prices were comparable to those in the States. The quality was very inferior. The styles of the shoes were fairly similar to ours of seven or eight years ago, except that almost all of the older women wore dark, sturdy, laced oxfords with a one-and-a-half-inch heel.

In one restaurant, which had originally been a camel stop, the rooms were like caves, uniquely and interestingly decorated with hanging rugs, wooden-slab tables, and a continuous low cushioned bench along a slowly moving wall. The rooms were clustered in a large circle and emptied in a courtyard, where the floor was cobblestone. A well with shrubs was in the center, and on one side Armenian music was playing. One member of our group snitched a bottle of vodka from one of the serving areas. I tried to help her hide it in a confiscated sweater from one of our members. I believed her group was nipping on the way back to the hotel, because when I met her back at the hotel disco she said she had dropped and broken the bottle. *Drats!* Our tour guide said the vodka was probably ours anyway. I said I thought so too, but it was much more fun pretending that it was stolen.

By this evening we were about a week and a half into the trip. Many people on the tour, including me, were having bouts of diarrhea. We were still enjoying the trip, but tempers were getting a little shorter. One time we were on a bus rounding corners on a mountain road. It was inky black outside except for the piercing lights of our bus as we barreled along. Quiet had set in as the narrow beam of the headlights rushed past the green of the countryside. We all had our private thoughts. All of a sudden voices, including mine, burst forth with "God Bless America," then "Anchors Away," "The Star-Spangled Banner," and a salute to the flag. OR a salute to the flag, and then the national anthem. Tears welled in the corners of my eyes. Here we were thousands of miles from home in a strange land of people who had been both our friends and our enemies. Some in the group had been quarrelsome, making unreasonable demands, asking inappropriate questions, and complaining about everything and everyone, but here at last we all touched in a solid front of love for the country that we were proudly and vociferously proclaiming as our very own.

Knowing how to manipulate situations in Russia took an incredible amount of firmness, tact, and quiet aggression. We were to end a five-hour bus trip at a beautiful restaurant overlooking a very large inland lake. The restaurant was over an hour's drive from our destination and another restaurant. The buses got separated on the way, and our driver got lost. The other two buses from our tour group arrived almost an hour before we did. It was about two thirty or three when we finally got to the restaurant. Instead of a trout dinner, our meal consisted of two slabs of brown bread between which a piece of cheese and a piece of fatty sausage had been placed. Tea could be had if anyone was lucky enough to catch a drink from a tray of tea sailing past.

Later in the women's room a tour group from Iowa let the cat out of the bag. They had arrived about an hour before us. They were told they would have a wait of one and a half to two hours before they could be served. The enterprising American guide bribed the restaurant manager with two cartons of cigarettes. They were served our food immediately. When we arrived we were told we would have to wait one and a half hours to be served. As the last of our group was straggling out after the brown bread and cheese, an enterprising member of our group who happened to have a jackknife confiscated an untouched plate of food from the plates being collected from the tables. A few of us picked fish off the bones after the main deboning had been done with the jackknife. At the last minute we found another untouched plate. I was the last to leave after wolfing down a few more bites of fish. It was delicious. It was mean but fun telling the others how good the fish was.

The women of Russia tended to be very heavy. There were almost no shapely, well-dressed women who looked as if they were past thirty years old. We were told that the American concept of liberated women in Russia was an illusion. They envied women who worked at home. They were the workhorses of the country. There wasn't enough money for them to stay at home, so they all worked. We heard the men lament in the hospitals about women who left to have babies. They were granted a year's leave and then could come back to the same job at the same pay. We found quota systems everywhere. People who were over their quota were rewarded, and people under their quota had to work harder. Stores that didn't meet their quota of sales had to stay open the last Sunday of the month. Doctors who saw extra patients over their quota made extra money.

The closest thing to our free enterprise system was called free markets. At the market the very small farms were represented by the farmers bringing in their extra bushel or bushels of whatever they grew; a few brought small animals they raised. Long wooden benches were divided into small areas of about three feet by three feet. Each farmer displayed his wares—tomatoes, carrots, cucumbers, radishes, grapes, fig fruit, pomegranates, green apples, peaches, pears, live scrawny chickens, and two live rabbits. Most of the fruit and vegetables were small in size. Extreme poverty by American standards was in evidence almost everywhere. Each farmer sold only one of anything. There were about eight 100-foot rows of the long wooden benches, with the farmers standing shoulder to shoulder. Both the men and women reflected hard work and very little money. Their clothes were very shabby. Their faces were weather-beaten, and their hands were coarse. Everything about the farmers seemed to indicate very hard physical labor.

Wherever we went there seemed to be very few men in their forties, fifties, and sixties. Women of those ages were everywhere, doing all sorts of work.

A few Russians wore crosses around their necks. Jesus Christ hung from some of the crosses. I asked one of the Russian tour guides for the meaning. She told me it meant nothing but a decoration and then added they were not worn to work. We were told the same thing by a Moscow University student who was majoring in engineering. He was a twenty-seven-year-old postgraduate student. We met him in a Moscow bar the last night we were there. He was from Tbilisi and was going back there when he graduated. He seemed shy and spoke in halting English. His friend had left the table for a few minutes, and when he came back the friend sat down and never acknowledged understanding English. When my husband asked the student if he wanted to come to the United States, a look of utter contempt curled at the corners of his friend's mouth. I mentioned the look to the Moscow student. The friend looked over at the Moscow student for a moment and again looked away. He was obviously very displeased with our conversation.

When we were taken around in the hospitals by the director, it seemed very strange to have him introduce us to men and women alike with the term "comrade."

Russia had approximately one hundred different dialects and languages among its people. I was not sure why our guides seemed to have no trouble being understood no matter where we went.

The 6,000-room hotel across from the Red Square in Moscow was the biggest hotel in the world. Sitting in the lobby was an older man who had what looked like a wedding band on his left hand. I got instantly curious because in Russia wedding bands were worn on the right hand. I pointed to his left ring finger and then to his right ring finger. He did not understand English. After talking to two of his friends, they figured out what my question was. He struggled to get the ring off and I looked away. When I looked back he was smiling and put the ring on the right ring finger. The knuckle was obviously too big to allow the ring over it. We both smiled in understanding, and then he replaced the ring on his left hand.

I asked our Russian guide if it would be okay to send the eleven-year-old boy I had met at the theater a pair of jeans for his twelfth birthday on October 11. She said that would be an insult unless it was the third or fourth gift I was sending him. When pressed for a suggestion, she said English or history books or the like, as there was a severe shortage of books written in English. A gift may be stopped at American customs or Russian customs. When a gift reached Russia, a slip of paper was sent to the recipient. The paper did not identify the gift, only that something had been sent. When he went to the pickup point with the slip of paper, the gift may not be there or it may not have reached the pickup point. When sending a gift to Russia, duty should be paid in the States so the Russian recipient does not have to pay the duty, which he may not be able to afford.

Russian children would hustle for popular street items, such as bubble gum, lighters, and pens. In turn, they had Mesha Russian bear pins or other pins, for which they bartered. Russian adults frequently tried to exchange rubles for dollars. One man on our trip exchanged a $100 bill for 300 or 400 rubles, which were worth $450 back in the States. The same two sons and father who exchanged American money for rubles sold jeans for 100 rubles. Coming into Russia they had each worn several pairs of jeans, which were much sought after in Russia. I heard that on another trip someone sold their used jeans for 200 rubles each. I didn't know how they got money back to the States. I could hear only a few of the words that were being exchanged between them and our tour guide. They were discussing getting money back to the States, but I couldn't hear enough to know what they were told. In customs their bags were gone over from stem to stern, and they got through okay.

Our American guide told us repeatedly, "Don't leave the country with more money than you came in with." Upon entering the country, a declaration was signed stating all jewelry, monies, and firearms that you were carrying. All legal exchanges of money were carefully documented on the back of the declaration, and then upon leaving the country another declaration had to be filled out stating the amount of jewelry, money, and arms that were being carried back across the border. Coming back into the United States, everything over three hundred dollars per person plus all foodstuffs and liquor must be declared.

Our clothing, shoes, and stockings were prized items. A few people gave items away. One woman gave a once-used woolen suit to one of the hotel desk ladies. Tears welled in her eyes as she kissed the donor. When we arrived in Russia and were going through customs, the luggage of only three of our eighty-six people was searched. Two of the people searched were men who sported beards. The one woman searched had a Polish name and wasn't surprised at being searched. We heard that some items confiscated were some books, magazines, and unlabeled medication or medication with someone else's name on the label. I was very curious, and much to the chagrin of my husband, who I had left behind holding our place in line, I went to the front of our line and stood against a counter that was not being used to see if anything exciting was going to happen to the people ahead of us in line. I was frequently given sidelong looks by the Russian customs agent and a Russian baggage clerk who was trying to break the line for the old Russian lady whose bags he was carrying. He finally went to the back of the line after much Russian chatter.

There was an old, very heavy Russian woman ahead of us. She was dressed in the usual dark shabby clothes, old dark sturdy oxfords, and a dark babushka. Her luggage consisted of one old locked, heavy cardboard suitcase and several assorted cloth and paper bags. A key for the locked suitcase could not be found. The bag was broken open. The customs agent went through every nook and cranny of her belongings. He didn't rush. He methodically went through approximately five handbags she had tucked into various places. Every small zippered pocket was opened. The linings of the handbags and bags alike were felt.

The customs agent never hesitated in handling items that I could see myself touching gingerly, such as rather disreputable-looking used shoes, which were carefully felt or shaken and added to the pile. All of her items were one at a time picked up, felt or shaken, looked at, and then dropped in the growing pile. The old lady was trying to cram handfuls of the items back into the bags, all the while chattering in Russian. Her tone was high-pitched and anxious. Many questions seemed to be asked of her as several pairs of used jeans and the used cheap handbags were being dumped. When they were finished with her, the last large pile of her paraphernalia was unceremoniously dumped on an adjoining counter. She crammed the remaining items helter-skelter back into any remaining space in her bags.

A few people in our group went through quickly, with only a cursory look at passports and items being brought into Russia. I was issuing frequent bulletins to my husband and a couple of other people from the front of the line. They started uneasily reviewing what might be confiscated. We didn't hold out much hope for several unlabeled pill bottles. Tension started building up. One person in our group had unlabeled medication for a heart condition. Next in line at the counter came a foreign language–speaking man. My husband said the man was Italian. His clothes were shabby but neat. He was about five feet six inches tall and quite stout. The customs agent, as he was chattering in a foreign language, immediately started to go through all of his belongings with the same rather slow, quiet intensity as he had used with the old lady's belongings. I had seen some fear on the old lady's face, but on this man's face there was raw fear. He and the woman he was with made jerky movements. Their eyes darted from one face to another as voices became higher-pitched, faster, and louder as the search went on.

The agent's voice never changed from his fast speaking in a fairly soft yet authoritative voice. The fly area of a pair of pants opened. Visible underneath was some uncut new material as that used to make men's pants. The agent quickly reached inside the pants, took out a small bolt of new material, and put it aside. He finished going through their suitcases. The agent talked to the baggage clerk next to me and to another man in back of the counter. The three Russians quickly gathered together and led the Italian man to a door in the wall about ten feet in back of the customs counter. All four quickly entered, and the door closed behind them. No one went in or out of the door for at least fifteen minutes. When they finally came out, the look of fear had left the old man's face. They were finished with him.

We went through without anything being opened. A white-haired sixty-eight-year-old Southern woman from our group was directly behind us. She was being held up, because instead of writing "None" under the question about whether you were carrying firearms into the country, she had just drawn a line. The agent wasn't letting her through. She didn't have a pen or reading glasses. I went back to help her. My husband was nervous, as agents seemed to be looking at us from everywhere. I asked the customs agent if I could borrow his pen. He said, "No, I need it." I rummaged in my bag and found a pen. I read the questions aloud to her in front of the customs agent and wrote in the proper word "None" under "Are you carrying any firearms?" The agent then accepted the form and let her through.

Our Russian tour guide told us that religious icons or items of historical consequence and some works of art would not be allowed out of the country. They would be confiscated at the border. The purchaser would be given a small numbered receipt and would continue to own the item. He or she could come and see it where it was warehoused. A woman from our group had a friend for whom she had agreed to take to one of her relatives in Russia a borgana coat, an artificial fur. When going through customs, she mentioned the coat to a Russian agent. The coat was held at the airport. On the day before we were to return to the United States, the Russian woman who was to receive the coat and one of our Russian tour guides went to the airport to try to get the coat. After approximately four hours of haggling and a call to the American donor, it was found out that a very high duty fee would have to be paid. It was finally decided to bring the coat back to the States. The woman carrying the coat back to the United States was directly in front of me going through Russian customs. The coat was loosely wrapped in brown paper and string. The paper had large Russian handwriting on it. This time, instead of the naive honesty that had led to the declaring of the coat and the intent of the bearer going in, it was surreptitiously kept under another coat hiding the Russian writing. Shortly after, it was on its way back to the States. Moscow had three airports, two domestic and one international. At all of the airports there was a separate seating area and a separate eating area for Intourists. The areas were much larger for the number of people served and more comfortable than the accommodations for the Russians. In at least two of the airports we had breakfast in special in-service dining rooms resplendent with white cloth napkins and fine china. The service and food matched that of their best restaurants.

When we arrived at the Erevan airport for our plane ride to Baku, the airport was socked in. Fog allowed us to see only a few feet. The lower level of the terminal was jammed with Russians of all ages and descriptions. The waiting area reeked of a combination of urine and various body odors. Bodies were everywhere. They had obviously been there for many long hours. Bags and bunched-up clothes littered the floor. Whenever a tiny space was available, a person assumed a semireclining position and a head nodded. Two chairs were pushed together under a staircase to form a makeshift cot, with feet hanging over one side and part of a head over the other. Crying, whining children made up part of the din. Wary, weary, and sometimes hostile looks were thrown our way as we were led through this assault to our visual, olfactory, and moral senses to a second-floor level, past Russians in poor-quality, heavy, rough coats standing at small tables measuring four by three feet across. They were eating hot dogs and thick coarse bread or very fatty sausage and cheese, with a mug for the beverage.

The poor Russians waiting in lines everywhere frequently seemed to have the stench of sausage and body odors about them. We went past the standing Russians to an in-service dining room. The tables were set with cloth napkins, fine china, two forks, two spoons, etc. Our breakfast, one of our better meals, had the little addition of fig jam to go on the bread and butter. There were hard-boiled eggs to go with the sausage and cheese. The sea of faces on the first floor, as seen from the second-floor landing, kept passing in front of me as we ate in their country, in the style, quality, and quantities that most of them would never experience.

I was at the head of the stairs, about to return to the first floor, when a commotion suddenly occurred farther down the stairs. A sixty-seven-year-old woman from our group seemed to just sit on the stairs. Her leg was broken above the ankle. Confusion and anxiety became the order of the day. A medical doctor and medic from our group took charge. I donated a Percodan. We couldn't get any water for her to take the pill. Now the decision had to be made as to what to do. She was traveling with her thirty-year-old boss and his sixty-year-old mother. The Russians wanted to send her back to Moscow and then back to the States. The pushy MD on our trip said, "Why? Strap her two legs together to form a natural cast, and take her on the plane with us to Baku. When we get there we can go to the hospital and get her a cast. Then she can continue on what for her is probably a once-in-a-lifetime opportunity. We can get her a pair of crutches in Baku." Of course this did not mean that he would help to carry her, which would be needed if she was to continue on the trip.

She was to be carried by the medic, another male passenger, and her boss. When the woman needed to be moved, he would appear and give the three men orders in crisp, no-nonsense tones and then disappear. He made another short appearance after a move to again give orders in the same tone of voice. He was traveling alone and was romancing a Southern belle who was traveling without her husband when he wasn't trying to move on other untapped American or Russian females. He frequently held court in hotel lobbies for female groups, giving them the latest medical bulletin on our problem passenger.

Our tour guide didn't know what to do. She had only had one such incident by which to judge what might be the best course of action. That incident involved a woman in her sixties who was traveling with her husband. She had fallen and broken a leg, and the leg had been cast. With the help of her husband, she kept up with the group even to visit the subway. In private I told the tour guide I would be afraid of a lawsuit, and if I were making the decision she would be sent back to the States. She asked, "What can I do if she wants to come along?" The MD was loud and overbearing. He sanctimoniously overrode objections and intimated selfish inconsideration for anyone who thought she should go back to the United States immediately. He told the woman with the break, "Of course you don't want to go back." He persevered, and she stayed. Our tour guide Julie and our Russian interpreter Tanya were paragons of virtue, patience, and perseverance. The front seats of planes and buses were reserved for her. Ambulances and staff were commandeered at airports. Our faithful three men carried her up and down plane ramps, as well as utilized whatever could be found in hotel lobbies, because no wheelchairs were ever available. All we ever saw was one set of crutches and no wheelchairs on any street or in the airports.

Baggage transporters were topped with a lobby chair and taken to the bus. She would then be carried from the bus to the lobby chair on top of the transporter and then on to a chair in the lobby or her bed. The reverse was needed to get her back on the bus. A soft cast had been put on in a Baku hospital. After the application of the cast, there were not supposed to be any problems unless she bore weight, according to our expert MD. She was being carried onto the bus. In trying to keep her balance getting through the door, she landed on her broken leg, and cries of pain escaped her. In Baku her boss had her measured for crutches. He and his mother had made a few efforts during the first day in Baku to find crutches. They couldn't find any. That evening they unceremoniously dumped the job on Julie, who was busy juggling eighty people through hotels, airports, sightseeing adventures, etc. Before we registered in a hotel, she would collect all of the passports and do whatever paperwork was needed along with the Russian interpreter for the hotel stay. The night before leaving a hotel, Julie passed out our passports in the dining room of the hotel. At each airport, even when we were traveling from one city to another inside Russia, our passports were checked.

As the trip progressed, the woman with the broken leg became more haggard. She spent a lot of time in her room. Even when Julie was finally able to locate a pair of crutches, she never used them. One evening she bought the group champagne for all of the waiting we had to do because of ambulances that took an hour to get to the airport, etc. As the trip progressed, her boss was beginning to snap at her. The decision to have her continue on this trip certainly seemed to have been the wrong one.

We were told by a reliable source that the Russians outside of Moscow would not be allowed to attend the Olympics—only tourists from other countries. We had no way to verify the validity of the information.

We saw no movie theaters anywhere in our travels. Televisions were rare. There were two being viewed by the desk women on the floor of the hotel where our room was located. Maybe that accounted for the sellout of many thousands of seats to circuses; ballet, jazz, and folk festivals; and other events. The floor women in hotels seemed to have living accommodations in rooms near their desks. We would often see the same usually stern, unresponsive face at 8:00 p.m. as we had seen at 8:00 a.m.

In most of the hotels in which we stayed, the din of traffic, as heard from the hotel room, was the same as that heard from a hotel room overlooking a Manhattan street. The cars were usually small four cylinders, compact, and functional, and they and the buses were frequently made in another country. In Baku, a vintage Cadillac with running boards sat in front of the hotel, along with a much newer Cadillac. They were the only two US-made cars that we saw. There were very few gas stations. We saw about three on the outskirts of cities. The lines waiting for gas usually consisted of several army vehicles, a couple of trucks, and six or seven cars. At night, vehicles were driven with only low beams. When passing a vehicle or on a country road, a pedestrian or rounding a corner bright lights were flashed on and then turned off again.

Public toilets were practically nonexistent. When a stop had to be made with another bus, where people had various stages of diarrhea, they were pointed to the back of a nearby building where there was an outhouse. They waited in line. The first woman who had gone inside came out and quickly proceeded to wipe feces off the sides of her shoes on the grass. The next woman to come out said, "I'm going to vomit," and directly proceeded to do so.

Soda machines were similar to ours in size only. There was one flavor and no throwaway cups. Two or three glasses were either on top of the machine or in the dispensing area. Someone wanting to buy soda picked up a glass and placed it upside down over a spot where a stream of water came up into the glass. The same glass was then placed right side up in the same area of the machine. A coin was placed in the machine, and soda went into the glass. The soda was consumed, and the glass was left to be used by the next person to come along. Beer was dispensed on the street. A large round drum-shaped barrel about five feet across was set into a framework with two wheels. On one end of the drum was a spigot. A woman sat next to the spigot dispensing jugs of beer. She washed and reused mugs after customers hurriedly drank beer and handed the mugs back to her.

I had expected, as in England and other countries, to see women dressed mostly in dark clothing. They weren't. Dresses were mostly made of cheap cotton in a bright flower pattern of one kind or another but were very conservatively cut. Pants on women were rarely seen except for jeans on young boys and girls alike. We priced some coats in a Russian store. A very inferior woman's coat of a nondescript material that looked like heavy rayon with poor quality fur at the neck cost the equivalent of over two hundred American dollars. Cheap cotton T-shirts were around fifteen dollars, and a Mesha teddy bear about one and a half inch high was over twenty-five dollars. Older people wore darker colors. Men's clothing tended to be even more conservative in cut and color than women's. There seemed to be no particular style in dress and shoes. We saw mostly functional, poor-quality, very limited supplies of everything.

In most of the stores, to buy the merchandise, the shopper had to pay and get a payment slip from a place in the store where everyone stood in line to get a slip. The slip was brought back to the counter where the goods desired were located. There a similar product was brought out from under a counter. At best most items were wrapped loosely in coarse paper. Usually items were placed in bags provided by the shopper.

On my return to my home in Babylon, New York, my first trip to a grocery store was a new treat. At the head of one of the fairly short aisles, I just stood for minutes feeling fantastic. The number of different items in most Russian grocery stores would be similar in count to one-half of one side of one aisle in an American grocery store. If only people could realize how very fortunate we were here in the United States.

At no time in all of our travels did we see a single fire hydrant or a single firehouse. We neglected to ask about this. In most of the hotels, the fire exit doors were locked. Several years ago at the Rossia Hotel in Moscow, many lives were lost because of locked fire exit doors. Almost all of the construction we saw was composed of cement slabs; nevertheless, locked fire exit doors gave a feeling of claustrophobia and unease.

The last night we spent in Moscow we wanted to see Russian folk dancing. The show had toured the United States. We had no tickets. Dinner was at six, and the show was to start at seven. Our hotel was on one side of the Kremlin Wall. The theater, which was a few blocks away, was on the other side of the wall. Cabs had to be ordered many hours before they would arrive unless someone was prepared to wait in endless lines. It was impossible at the end of a rushed dinner at about a quarter to seven to walk to the theater in time for the show. If someone was late, they would not be seated.

We went over to a cab parked in front of the hotel that had only parking lights on and asked the driver if he would take us to the theater. I had copied the theater's name from the ticket of someone in our group. We knew legitimate cab fare was approximately one-half of one ruble, or about seventy-five cents. The driver said the ride would cost five rubles. My husband angrily repeated, "Five rubles," and stalked off. The cab driver had smilingly pointed up the hill. We went about a hundred feet and, sure enough, there was a long line waiting by a cab sign. Five minutes later not one cab had appeared, and there were none in the vicinity. I suggested offering the original cab driver we had spoken to two American dollars. We scrounged up one dollar bill and four quarters. We went back down the hill and offered the driver our American money. Sure enough, off we went.

When we got to the theater, which was actually inside the Kremlin Wall, people were already rushing to go inside. And we had no tickets! At the door we asked a Russian woman where we could get tickets. We couldn't understand her, and she couldn't understand us. I started asking people if they understood English. Finally, one person in a group of three men said yes. He suggested we come back the next day. We told him that was impossible because by the next day we would be gone. He said the only other thing we might try was to go outside the front door and see if we could find someone with tickets to sell. Here we were with only a few more minutes before curtain time, and we still had no tickets. We went outside. There were few people standing outside. We asked several people, who just shrugged with no comprehension.

Finally, a man responded to the word *"billet."* He pulled two tickets from his pocket. We thought he was a scalper. We kept asking, "How much?" He seemed to be giving us tickets. We showed him a ten-ruble bill. Finally, he pulled a five-ruble bill out of his pocket and took our ten. The tickets read two rubles, sixty kopeck each, or a little over five rubles. He not only was not a scalper but had lost a little on the deal. Our seats turned out to be good ones on the second tier but separated. It didn't matter. The person who sold us the tickets turned up and sat next to us. We speculated that probably someone he was expecting hadn't shown up. Interestingly this was the first show that did not show struggling and revolution, aside from the show we had seen of the American jazz musicians.

At the circus before every act there was a depiction of struggle. There was military-sounding music and harsh-sounding words as some form of red star or hammer and sickle were displayed, from headdresses to flags, etc. The circus was a magnificent one-ring affair with many variations of a balancing act. The entire show was preceded by a march from one side of the circus tent to the other of representatives from each of the Russian-conquered nations—Poland, Hungary, Czechoslovakia, etc.—as each of their music, in turn, was played over the loudspeakers.

Wherever we went, the same message was repeated—there was great honor in serving and, if need be, in dying for your country. The best medical care the country had to offer was given in VA hospitals. Soldiers past and present were given preferential treatment. In our visit to the last hospital, where the one elevator took only six people at a time, we were told that we were the first Americans to visit that hospital. At the end of the tour we were asked if there was anything else we wanted to see. Several times in other hospitals we had asked to see patient charts and nurses' stations. What better way to get a good idea of what kind of care was given than to see the amount of paper work for each patient? After all, I felt sure that nobody took X-rays or gave out medications without charting.

The hospital director seemed to have a difficult time understanding the request. I changed the words around a little and tried again. Finally, he smiled and led us down the hall. He gestured toward a nurse sitting at a small wooden desk. There was one shallow wooden drawer in the middle of the desk. It measured roughly two feet by one and a half feet with a depth of about two inches. Inside were four or five manila folders with a little paper work inside. Other papers were loose inside the drawer. The drawer was only about half full. The drawer serviced one hospital wing, as did the medicine cabinet next to it. The medicine cabinet had glass doors and resembled the medicine cabinets seen in our very old movies. Three or four medication bottles could be seen on the upper shelves, while the bottom two shelves held thermometers and other paraphernalia.

Someone asked if circumcision was mandatory. The answer was "No, only if it is medically indicated."

Whether we were in the hospitals or in the hotels, there were very few, if any, wall decorations. The few pictures were frequently of Lenin, struggle, and/or war. Walls were usually painted in the neutral colors of white, off-white, and yellow. We saw wallpaper only once. When we returned to Moscow, wallpaper was on the wall of our room.

The newsstands in hotel lobbies carried a very limited selection of newspapers. One newspaper was in English, three or four were in a foreign language, and a few foreign language magazines looked from the covers to be mostly of a political nature. In addition, there was a selection of approximately six or seven postcards that cost forty cents to airmail to the States.

In most of the cities, nightlife seemed to be very limited. By eleven o'clock, the Rossia closed its last small bar. After a theater performance in Moscow, we went to the American Embassy. Two Russian soldiers stood on each side of the front arched entrance. A little gesturing and talking got us nowhere. An American came out and led us through the courtyard to what seemed like back stairs that led to a small disco run by American Marines. The disco had a bar that was about fifteen feet long. There were approximately eleven tables that each seated four people. The tables lined two sides of a ten-by-ten-foot dance floor. Loud disco music was playing, and there were very few patrons.

The actions of the American men were in sharp contrast to the men of Moscow. Not only were they bold in the streets, but nightlife reflected their almost gay abandon. On hotel and restaurant dance floors, boys and young men moved up and down to the music in a rhythmless frenzy, sometimes with women and sometimes with each other.

On one of the tours we saw Russian boys and young men practicing ski jumps. It was in Moscow on the bank of a river. Across the river we could see the huge stadium being built for the 1980 Olympics. A type of pulverized plastic was being used for snow. The ski jump was frequently sprayed with water. Far off at the base of the jump was sand. The skiers jumped every couple of minutes. They had on the traditional blue long-sleeved, long-legged sweats and all the skiing paraphernalia. In the air the young men seemed to gracefully fly in an arched descent. The younger boys seemed to be in a more stiffened and defensive posture of the less experienced during their long aerial descent.

Before Lenin's rise to power, the literacy rate of the country was said to have been 20 percent. The literacy rate was now proudly stated to be 100 percent.

On the last day in Russia, I very much wanted to see the inside of the mausoleum that housed Lenin's tomb. It was in the Red Square directly across the street from the Rossia hotel, where we were staying. After all, he is to many or most of the Russian people the equivalent of their God and that is how they treat all references to him.

We had been given two extra days in Russia because there was a problem at New York's JFK Airport. There were no other people who had a final New York destination, so we were left to our own devices. Looking in the direction of the high metal gate that opened to the Red Square, we saw a very large group of Russian people. We decided to try to infiltrate the group and be as inconspicuous as possible. It was quite cold, and people were bundled in dark, heavy, worn coats, hats, scarves, and gloves. There was no way that our American clothing and my being taller than most Russian women did not make us stand out. In addition, we had not been able to get a pass that would allow us past the guards at the gate. There was some fear. After all, we did not have our savvy guide to lead us.

We stayed as close to the middle of the group as possible and somehow made it past the gate where several other lines had formed. One line was for the women, and the other line was for the men. We clung to each other. Neither the Russians around us nor the green-uniformed police spoke any English. A policeman motioned toward a green bus nearby as he tried to take my purse. One of the things they were looking for was cameras. I got a bit frantic, shaking my head no while opening my purse so he could see no camera inside. I repeated rather loudly, "Nothing, nothing." He finally let us go.

Off in the distance a very long line of Russians were being moved very slowly into the building housing Lenin's body. Much to our consternation, even across the Red Square we could see that every person was being searched. My husband had a rather small camera on his person, which he had managed to hide when we first entered. When questioned on entering the square he vigorously shook his head indicating no. We figured that what might work was if we were viewed as clingy, holding hands and/or with my hand in his pocket. It was nerve-racking. The line was so long, and it moved so slowly as everybody was carefully searched. What would happen if they found his camera? Our passports were back at the hotel. I was not sure what worked, but there we were going down the steps of Lenin's tomb. There were stiff regal-looking guards on every other step and lining the walls around the narrow walkway of the large glass display case surrounding his body. Lenin's face was a rather chalky white. I whispered something to my husband and was quickly silenced with a hiss from one of the guards.

An interesting historical fact was that one of the tombstones along the inner wall of the Red Square and on the same side as Lenin's mausoleum was that of an American. I did not get his name.

At a theater performance in Russia, I had been able to get two Russian students' addresses, with the intention of starting correspondence between Russian and American students. After all, what could be more positive than trying to establish détente between two countries that seemed to be in a never-ending jockeying position for indications of superiority?

I brought my notes on Russia and the addresses to the Babylon grade-school principal, Mr. Smith.

> September 20, 1979
>
> Dear Mr. Smith,
> Here are some notes in case any of your teachers might be interested in starting correspondence with an eleven-year-old boy. He and his teacher spoke no English, so we spoke through the cheerful efforts of a student nearby who translated from English to Russian and from Russian to English.
> Theresa Santmann

I did not hear from the principal for several weeks. Finally, when I called him, I was told that the request for possibly starting correspondence between Russian and American students had been given to the school lawyer. The lawyer said no, as the request was politically incorrect.

Chapter 24

Building a Second Nursing Home

The year was 1991. I thought that building another nursing home would be an interesting challenge. My daughter, Theresa Annette, who was a Johns Hopkins University and Wharton School of Business graduate, had come back to the area as the assistant administrator of the Little Flower Nursing Home. I was the administrator. Between the two of us, surely we could move such a project along.

I called a friend of mine who worked for the New York State Health Department. I told him about everything I owned in the world and asked him if he thought that my building another nursing home was a feasible idea. He laughed and gave me an affirmative answer.

The immediate questions from the New York State Health Department were: (1) "Is there a need for more beds?" and (2) "In what area of New York State does that need exist?" Other questions arose under local government regulations regarding proper zoning on the land to be acquired, and the acreage that would accommodate state and local government regulation.

I located several properties in the area that had been identified by the health department as in need of additional nursing home beds. A man named Commissioner Miles was very familiar with local codes and regulations in the region, and he immediately could tell me

151

what my prospects were of getting approval on a particular property. His answer was always no. Finally, I asked him if he knew of any land that was properly zoned and of adequate acreage. He advised me of a 3.5-acre parcel of land on Broadway in Sayville that met the necessary criteria. On checking on the owners of the property, I discovered there were three different owners, one of which was the Mets management corporation. The taxes on the property had not been paid for several years. I made a number of inquiries, and finally many months later the land was put up for auction by Suffolk County. What an exciting time. I was prepared to go to $400,000, which was the amount I had calculated as the most I should pay to continue the venture.

The auction was a two-day affair held in a large auditorium. The auctioneers sat on a stage facing the attendees, who were seated in many rows facing the stage. A small catalog was available, which described the many different pieces of land that were to be auctioned, as well as the upset price, which was the lowest amount of money that would be accepted for that particular piece, and the order of the sale of the items. I sat through most of the first day's sale knowing that the land I wanted was probably not coming up until later during the second day, based on the listing in the catalog. After a period of time, it became obvious that some real estate people from the back of the room were the big players in the fast pace set by the auctioneer.

At last the next day came. I got to the building rather early and sat in the same seat I was in the day before. This became one of the most exciting days of my life, as I kept track of when the sale of the property was coming up. Finally, it was the very next number. I let the real estate people make the first and second bids. By then the amount being bid was about $300,000. I started at about $325,000. Among us the bid rose quickly to $380,000. Finally, with a fast-beating heart, I made the bid of $400,000. Thankfully the auctioneer brought his hammer down rather quickly on my final bid, and at last the land was mine. Now if I could get the title cleared, I could start the next part of this project. Every one of the people listed as owners had to be notified of its sale at the auction, and if any one of them came forward with the overdue tax money, the sale became null and void. At last I got a Torrens title.

The challenges faced during the building of the Petite Fleur Nursing Home at times seemed insurmountable. The land was outside the boundaries of a sewer district, which mandated the connection to a sewage treatment plant or the building of such a plant under the guidelines of the Department of Environmental Conservation. Finding where the DEC offices were located was only the beginning. There seemed to be no way for me to talk to anyone, so finally I called their main number and asked the person answering the phone who was the person I should be talking to about building a sewage treatment plant. She told me the person's name and then told me that a red-haired man would be coming out of a meeting shortly. His door opened to the main lobby. He was the man I was looking for. I followed her directions and sat in the lobby of the main building, waiting for the red-haired man to come out of a meeting room. Finally, such a man appeared. I quickly went over to him and identified that the person I needed to see was the person who would be able to give me some direction in the need for a sewage treatment plant for the building of a nursing home. He quickly stated he wasn't the appropriate person and gave me another man's name.

I managed to get an appointment with someone to start the long road to approval to build the sewage treatment plant. There were so many questions. Where were all of the other treatment plants in the area? Would I be made to tie into any one of them? There wasn't adequate space between a proposed plant and neighboring properties, based on the calculations of the DEC. The only way to get their approval was to make a formal presentation of an architectural change to shorten one of the wings on the original design, which was to be addressed by including a lower level of the building to cover the needed space. The questions and answers continued until finally the Petite Fleur Nursing Home was officially opened in October 1993.

The Little Flower Nursing Home was comfortably running in the black. The Petite Fleur Nursing Home was, as all start-up businesses are, in need of working capital until the corner was turned and it became a viable enterprise. Initially, mortgaging my home and properties covered the start-up costs.

For at least a few years the banks on Long Island had been addressing local business needs with a rather free hand until they seemed to tighten the money flowing to Long Island businesses at the same time they seemed to be opening the door to the European markets. Initially the bank I had been doing business with for many years had promised adequate funding of working capital for the Petite Fleur Nursing Home.

Hillary Rodham Clinton was just starting to push her health-care initiative. Her proposal to insure all Americans had been done behind closed doors without one health-care professional in attendance. What happened next was that all banks were closing their doors on health-care projects that were not wholly collateralized by other property owned.

I needed approximately $1.5 million of working capital for the Petite Fleur Nursing Home. Bank of America, which had promised the appropriate coverage, now demanded collateral based on everything I owned, complete with appropriate certificates of occupancy, some of which were over fifty years from date of issuance. The bank still dragged their feet on making the needed money available.

Next I went to all the local banks, asking for the needed monies. Finally, Apple Bank agreed to loan me $400,000. When I made the Apple Bank offer known to Bank of America, I was told that if I took the four hundred thousand dollars from Apple Bank, they would withdraw any possibility of my getting the needed money from them. A few days later on Friday afternoon at approximately three o'clock, I had run out of money and would not be able to cover the payroll of the Little Flower Nursing Home and the Petite Fleur Nursing Home. I called Bank of America, sobbing about the fact that I couldn't meet the payrolls of either facility. They finally agreed to let me borrow the four hundred thousand dollars from Apple Bank.

Time went on. The Apple Bank monies were quickly being dispersed, while covering the two payrolls, and Bank of America was still dragging their feet on a loan. The thought came to me, *I must bring my need directly to the head of the bank if I have any chance of getting the money I need to meet the two payrolls until Petite Fleur Nursing Home is able to meet its own payroll.*

I called the bank and finally was able to get a meeting with the president of the bank at its headquarters on the northwest corner of the Long Island Expressway and Route 110. The president's office was on the top floor of the building. It was very intimidating, with its elegance and grandeur. There was a long conference table, with its many chairs, a gun rack in one corner, an impressive desk, and accoutrements, with a spacious seating area.

I brought along the accountant who serviced both nursing homes, hoping he would help to make my case for the needed monies. The bank's New England branch managers were in attendance and added negative input to help negate the loan. I was pleading my case, when finally the person with whom I had been dealing for many months, who had been my nemesis, was the last to come into the room. Somehow it seemed to me that this was somehow designed to put the final blow on the possibility of my getting the needed loan. I smiled and enthusiastically told him how very nice it was to see him.

I got the loan!

Chapter 25

Traveling with Nanna

There was nothing ominous in the sparkling blue skies and gentle, warm winds blowing over MacArthur Airport. It was Saturday, January 14, 1994. My grandson Mathew, barely three, and I were making our first joint venture to a home I owned in Boca Raton, Florida. Our scheduled two-and-a-half-hour flight turned into a six-and-a-half-hour marathon, eliciting anxiety, frequent boredom, and heart-pounding fright.

At noon, the scheduled departure time, the passengers and luggage were all on board when an announcement came over the intercom: "There will be a delay. We are waiting to take on extra fuel as the Fort Lauderdale Airport is closed due to rain, poor visibility, and high winds with tornado warnings. We may be flying to North Carolina or to Nassau in the Bahamas. We have to have enough fuel to be able to change our flight plan while we are airborne." The anxious grumbling heightened in intensity as the wait lengthened and temperatures in the plane's cramped quarters rose. Some passengers who wanted to disembark were told they could, but their luggage would have to go to Fort Lauderdale. No one got off the plane.

Finally, at one thirty we were airborne. Frequent announcements with the latest weather data, as well as changing decisions on our next destination, came over the intercom in a crisp English accent. "The Fort Lauderdale Airport is still closed. In case there is a chance we can get clearance to circle until we can land in Fort Lauderdale or if we need to fly to a distant airport, we will take on extra fuel in North Carolina." The first hour's activity was mostly a movie playing on the overhead screen while drinks and meals were served. The comforting drone of the engines furnished background noise.

Suddenly we fell many feet. What had been our secure and steady environment became a buffeted, balking hunk of metal. Could these wings that now looked so fragile stay riveted to the body? Seat belts were quickly tightened. I clung very hard to Mathew. Armrests were grasped so tightly, white knuckles were evident as anxious looks flashed about. Some children cried. Our plane was overloaded with fuel. Fuel trails could be seen coming from the wings as some fuel was jettisoned so we could land in what was now a definite destination, a North Carolina airport.

The time on the ground in North Carolina seemed endless. We were not allowed to disembark. We were told that again refueling to the max would be critical, as we still didn't know how long, when again airborne, we would be forced to stay aloft.

Mathew was sleeping. His new white sneakers were on an accommodating passenger's lap as his head rested in my lap. War stories were exchanged. The man in the seat in front of us told of going out of the Fire Island Inlet in a nineteen-foot boat to a fishing destination fifty miles away with one motor and with no means of communication.

I shared a story of taking my forty-foot boat into New York Harbor and miscalculating the hour of darkness on returning. I was caught in the ocean outside of the Fire Island Inlet after dark. Thank goodness my recuperating husband had no idea of the imminent danger of our situation. Finally, off in the distance, in the darkness of the ocean came the recognizable lights of a fishing boat that I gratefully followed through the inlet. The husband of the woman on my right was a pilot. I had a pilot's license, so we could share the problems with what was the dreadfully short east–west runway at the now-closed Zahn's Airport in Farmingdale.

Many more stories were told as time wore on. At last we were airborne. The announcements continued. The airport in Fort Lauderdale still had not reopened, and many planes were backed up trying to land. We were going to fly down the west coast of Florida, and then that was changed to the east coast. Finally, the announcement came that Fort Lauderdale Airport had just been reopened. We were the first plane to get permission to land and would be ahead of all of the others in various holding patterns at other locations.

By now Mathew was awake. I was reading *101 Dalmatians* to him. Suddenly we were again in the throes of another storm and being tossed about. I tried to keep reading, but Cruella de Vil bounced from the top to the bottom of the page and back again. Mathew never cried but started to get very restless. Thank God for barf bags. All of my neighbors were trying to help. One's barf bag was stuck closed with gum, and another couldn't find hers. Kleenex came from someone else. We all cheered and clapped when we landed.

On the return trip, when Mathew was allowed into the cockpit and the pilot and copilot were trying to strike up a conversation, all he had to say was "On the other big airplane with wheels, I threw up."

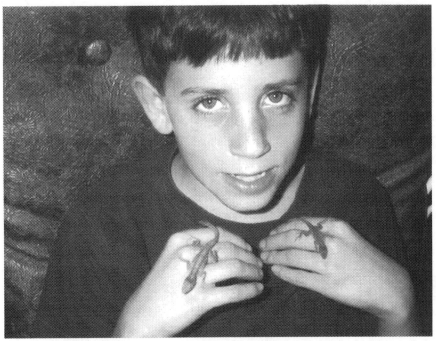

Grandson Mathew at grandmother Theresa's Florida home making friends with tiny reptiles.

Mathew feeding a goat at a Florida game farm.

Chapter 26

Thanksgiving with Nanna

I had promised the three kids—Mathew, who turned three two days before Thanksgiving; Catherine, six years old; and eight-year-old Randy—a turkey for Thanksgiving.

We were in Boca Raton, Florida, on a one-week vacation in 1994. Time flew by. It was eight thirty on Wednesday night, and I still had no bird. We all tumbled into a grocery store called Publix. The kids might not know the difference between a fancy spread or a plain meal, but they would know if they hadn't been served a bird of one kind or another. The store was going to close soon, so my selections had to be done in the next forty-five minutes.

The frozen section still had turkeys of all sizes. It would be impossible to get a turkey thawed and then cooked for eating tomorrow. I spied a small glass-enclosed display case with, of all things, several ready-to-bake stuffed birds. One called a roasting hen seemed like the safest bet. Not a soul, as in store personnel, was around to get the bird out for me. I called on a nearby phone and still got no response. With the encouragement of a fellow conspiratorial shopper passing by, I got the bird out of the case myself. Added to this treasure were several sweet potatoes, a can of cranberry sauce, and a Mrs. Smith's frozen coconut custard pie. We were the last customers to leave the store.

Thanksgiving came. Maybe I could take the kids to the Hallandale Fair for a few hours and make the day truly festive. There were thrilling rides made to elicit squeals of delightful fear, as well as rides that took us high in the sky to marvel at the sparkling lights of Hallandale spread out before us. Food booths of all descriptions were everywhere. Some seemed as if they had been transplanted from New York's Little Italy festival. There were hamburgers, boiled corn, caramel apples, and popcorn, but the new delight for all of us was elephant ears, which was a pie-shaped raised doughnut with available add-ons, from powdered sugar to creams and fruit mixtures.

There were three eighty-five-by-forty-foot tents. One tent had many rows of fowl, from turkeys to pigeons. Over the turkeys was a sign: "Eat pork for Thanksgiving." Another tent had plants, and the third tent had cows, newborn suckling piglets, donkeys, and goats with their little ones. We were on our way out when we spied a stage where kids from seven to sixteen were jabbing and kicking in a display of karate skills. Of course we had to stop for that. We didn't get home till almost ten o'clock, with half of our crew asleep and all of us stuffed.

Friday was going to be our Thanksgiving. The day started with the children having a late and large breakfast, so certainly they weren't going to be hungry till midafternoon.

The directions on the chicken read, "Roast at 325 degrees for 1 to 1½ hours." My planning was really quite good. The chicken and several white potatoes covered lightly with aluminum foil would go in first at about one in the afternoon, to be followed in a half hour by the sweet potatoes. When that feast was ready to come out, the pie could be popped in at 400 degrees. In addition, the canned corn and Tuesday's French bread, along with cranberry sauce, would round out the details of our holiday feast.

I got an inkling that all might not work out quite as planned when I unwrapped the bird from its covering of Saran Wrap. Inside was the pecan and apple stuffing enclosed in its own bag. I had seen similar-looking concoctions coming out of a cement mixer, except for the specks of orange. The outlined dressing ingredients had a positive statement about the vegetable contents, so I assumed the tiny orange-colored specks were bits of carrots.

Even the oven complained. I couldn't get the darn thing from going off with a piercing rattling sound every fifteen minutes that would have put any $10 alarm clock to shame.

By two o'clock every one of the children had registered various degrees of complaints, ranging from the three-year-old's "I'm hungry" to the six-year-old's "I'm starving."

The bird had been in the oven for an hour with the meat thermometer stuck in its middle. By two o'clock the thermometer had not changed very much. It was not looking good. All that was ready were the baked sweet potatoes, the heated canned corn, the two-day-old French bread, and the oranges we had just picked from our neighbor's yard and squeezed for juice. Maybe this would quiet them down for a little while.

By three o'clock, the two o'clock feeding had worn off. I could not keep them contained any longer, and the alarm was driving me crazy. The meat thermometer still wasn't up to the numbers section, and the kids were letting me know in no uncertain terms that they were still very hungry. *Okay, here goes.* The hen's aluminum cover came off. When I wrestled the leg down to start serving, the inside of the leg showed pink meat of the not-cooked-enough variety. *Ugh, not done!* Maybe the white breast meat was done. The point of a sharp knife barely pierced what was by now a chicken in a stiff leathery encasement.

Thank goodness there was enough white meat cooked sufficiently to feed three hungry kids. I didn't think they realized that the heavy clump of dressing on each of their plates was barely edible, but when they mixed it with the cranberry sauce, what did kids know? The chicken portion left for me was a drumstick. It was the most rubbery piece of chicken I had ever gnawed upon.

Next year, I didn't care how crowded the restaurants were, it wouldn't be "to Grandma's house we go."

*Grandson Mathew
Grossman at Nanna
Theresa's barbecue,
1994.*

*Babylon village
western barbecue
at 66 Cedar Lane,
Babylon. Partying
Hans Lewald
in white shirt,
October 23, 1994.*

*Babylon Village
barbecue pig roast
with Divina Leitch
and two workers,
October 23, 1994.*

Chapter 27

Babylon Village Republican Club Western Barbecue

For days the sky had been intensely blue, with puffy white clouds and gentle warm winds. A light drizzle started early in the morning of Sunday, October 23, 1994.

It couldn't rain, because between three o'clock and seven o'clock, the Babylon Village Republican Club western barbecue was being held at my home on Cedar Lane in Babylon, New York. But rain it did.

By one o'clock Billie Hill Jr.'s three blue-and-white tents had been properly secured. Even as the tents were being set up, Babylon Village trustee Ralph Scordino and Bob McGrath had a hind quarter of cow pierced, rotating, and already sizzling over a bed of red-hot coals.

Would anyone come to a western line dance held outside in pouring rain under dripping tents?

By two o'clock event chairman Hanse Lewald had western saddles hung over bales of hay. Cornstalks decorated poles. Orange pumpkins and yellow, purple, and white mums were everywhere.

The rain kept coming. There were anxious moments, but then a few minutes after three o'clock President Hugh Leitch was welcoming the hearty souls coming in twos and threes. Among them were Owen Johnson, Phil Boyle, Matte Fitzgibbons, Gay Lazeto, Fran Brown, Andy Tufari, and Mayor Don Conroy.

Under a tent where a dance floor had been set up, the Hi Country Western Band throbbed out its lively high-stepping sounds while Long Island western instructor Sherry Palencia and the red-shirted country club dancers enticed many guests to join them in the rhythmic line dance.

Much to everyone's surprise, Steve Sacchi delighted everyone by picking up a guitar and belting out several western songs, sounding like a professional hoedown artist.

One of the tents had been set up with many tables decked out in red-and-white gingham tablecloths. There were dried ears of corn, along with green, orange, and yellow gourds forming decorative centerpieces.

Throughout the evening, Paul Scordino could be seen circulating among the tents, poking at the accumulated pockets of water collecting in the overhang so the extra weight of the water wouldn't pull down the tents. Water cascaded to the ground in sheets with the wind, sometimes carrying some of the water to the backs of those seated too close to the edge of the tents.

The dance floor became slippery. Squishy and gradually deepening mud and water accumulated in the several feet between the tents until someone thought of spreading bales of hay in the slushiest areas, and the merriment went on. Western boots became wet to the ankles. The bottoms of the broomstick skirts had inches of water markings. Most skirts and blouses had various degrees of dampness.

Seen in the crowd were town leader Frank Volz, Frank Aprea, Republican Zone leader of the village of Babylon, Herb Hemindinger, the Skillens, the Bergers, Donna of the Beacon, the Kochs, and the Smiths.

A harrowing tale of the day before the party surfaced, as told by the attending artist Peter Zorzenon. He was the artist of the ten-foot metal rendering of an Indian on a horse and the eagles spreading their wings over the brick stations of each of the two driveways on the property.

Peter was twenty miles offshore fishing in his twenty-two-foot boat when a rogue wave rolled the boat upside down. He was thrown into the cold water. He dove into the water's pitch-black depths under the boat, groping to try to find flares. He had no success. No boats passed for over seven hours. It wouldn't be very long before darkness and probable death yawned in his face. Finally, a boat came close enough for its passengers to hear and see him, and he was rescued.

By the next evening all traces of the party were gone. It was a little sad. Planning and preparation took so long, and then it rained as the party joyfully sloshed along. All too soon it was finished and already just a happy memory.

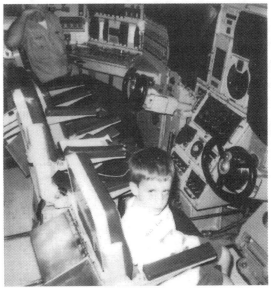

Mathew at the controls of the USS Oklahoma City submarine.

Grandson Mathew with a sailor next to the USS Oklahoma City submarine docked at a Fort Lauderdale marina. It was there to give the surviving children of the April, 1995 bombing of the federal building in Oklahoma City a submarine ride into the Atlantic Ocean.

Chapter 28

Submarine USS *Oklahoma City*

Writing about this marvelous experience so many years later did not lend itself to as much clarity as I might have liked. The year was 1995, and here it was 2012. I had traveled to Florida with my grandson Mathew Grossman to my house in Boca Raton. Mathew was four years old and a great travel companion.

He stayed in good spirits even under rather trying circumstances. I had a forty-foot yacht named *Wicky Two*. No matter the weather, rain or shine he remained my number-one mate. Even if the night was going to be very cold, if I had promised an overnight in the *Wicky Two* while it was docked at my house in Babylon, New York, that required the inclusion of one large and one small dog, I had to keep my promise. Wherever I took him, such as the Lion Country Safari, the dolphins at the Miami Seaquarium, or the intercoastal waterway for a day of fishing, he made the experience fun.

I was taking Mathew on an adventure that took us down the main highway from Boca Raton south toward Miami. We were in the Fort Lauderdale area when I looked left and saw, off in the distance toward the ocean, a rather odd-looking outline that did not resemble any that I might have seen in the past. I followed the sighting as closely as I could. A sign read, "Warning: No Trespassing. Unauthorized personnel will be subject to arrest and prosecution. Port Everglades Authority PSD." I was never stopped until I was parked close to what turned out to be a nuclear-powered US submarine. What a wonderful surprise. We were welcomed with warmth and goodwill from the stationed navy personnel.

The submarine was in port in order to take the surviving children from the Oklahoma City bombing that had partially destroyed the Alfred P. Murrah Federal Building. The next day they were to be warmly greeted and honored and then taken out of the inlet nearby to the ocean, where the periscope was to be raised, as they were shown the different areas of the submarine.

Mathew and I were shown through the many areas of the submarine. Mathew sat in the opening of the housing for torpedoes, which looked into a periscope viewing. He sat in a control chair with his hands on the steering wheel in front of a panels of controls.

The following are the notes I took while on board the submarine:

- Sailor's tour of duty: three to four years
- Submarine stationed in Norfolk, Virginia
- Crew: 140; officers: 4
- 360 feet long
- Everything redundant (e.g., two periscopes, on surface can see about nine miles)—"Now I see two boats through this"
- Sonar dome made out of fiberglass
- Keel laid: January 4, 1984
- Launched: November 2, 1985
- Commissioned: July 9, 1988
- Nuclear-powered
- Only 70 subs left, was 140
- In New London, Connecticut; Norfolk, Virginia; Kings Bay, Georgia; Bangor, Washington; Pearl Harbor
- United States responsible for supporting US bases, verifying sea lanes stay open.
- Bosnia has Russian soldiers working in cooperation with US peacekeeping
- Sonar display is 360 degrees except baffle area; on and recording 24 hours a day
- Tactical readiness, make sure ship is capable of doing everything it should be doing in war
- Orange torpedo practice, wire-guided

- Missile, just enough fuel to get away from ship
- Steel wire (protective) to be inside like piano wire, thinner than telephone wire; coil inside feeds out
- Mark 48 torpedo—one power kill—orange retrieve—run out of gas—float to surface; another boat scoops it up
- Battery good three hours
- Diesel works generator rig for reduced electrical, can turn enough to get home eight-and-one-eighth-inch piston
- The back end of submarine protrudes in a sliver of black rubberized skin placed like an alternating patchwork quilt with white projecting under that 37 with progressing numbers 6,5,4,3,2 on both sides and the curving front going toward
- Forward compartment was approximately 75 ft. submerged, then gradual bellying out to the sail, fills with water, two smaller periscopes, and green radio antenna
- Three hatches, escape trunk pressure (e.g., put in 10 lbs. more pressure inside so easy to open)
- Inspection every 12 to 18 months
- Always training

Chapter 29

On the Town

The evening of September 30, 1997, started uneventfully. Four friends—Jackie Brucia, Theresa Santmann, Theresa DelToro, and Judy Skillen—were on the Long Island Railroad heading for Penn Station to enjoy a night on the town.

First we had dinner at Tatou on Fiftieth Street, which proved to be a gourmet delight. Paper-thin meat was served on birds' nests of frosty lettuce, and desserts with different-colored sauces were twirled into attractive designs. The ceilings were high, with a crystalline chandelier throwing off bits of light.

Two of us were going to see *Show Boat*, and the other two were going to see *Beauty and the Beast*. Of course, chatting kept us at the restaurant past a reasonable time to get to the theater. On leaving the restaurant, we ran into a delay. The street was blocked off. Police were trying to restrain the loudly screaming marchers carrying signs. The police appeared to be trying to move the marchers along at a more rapid pace than the marchers wanted to go.

The theater was already being darkened for the start of the play as we rushed in.

By the time we were ready to start our trek home, it was nearing one o'clock. There didn't seem to be many people at Penn Station. On seeing the sign "Long Island Railroad," we asked the first uniformed person we saw, "When is the next train to Babylon?"

The answer was "There are none till morning. You will have to take the subway to Jamaica and a train to Babylon from Jamaica."

The looks of horror were evident on all of our four faces. One of us said, "If we take the subway, my husband will never let me come back to the city." My response was "The last time I took the subway, twenty years ago, I was accosted." We churned, trying to come up with a suitable response to our dilemma. We realized it would be next to impossible to get a cab to take us all the way to Babylon. Someone mentioned an overnight stay at a motel, but several of us had nine o'clock commitments in Babylon the next morning.

Though filled with almost overwhelming apprehension, we started toward the subway. There were very few people using the subway. We wended our way through the seemingly never-ending, rather dimly lit tunnels of the subway. Every transient, as well as every young man under thirty, was perceived as a possible attacker. What somewhat eased our choking anxiety was the sight of railroad employees at almost every turn. They were highly visible with their portable phones and yellow-and-orange dayglow vests. Some passengers in the subway car looked a bit disreputable. Mostly the trip to Jamaica was uneventful, and we gradually breathed more easily.

It was nearing three in the morning when we finally boarded the train at Jamaica for Babylon. At that time, the chatting among us had become sporadic, and occasionally one of us nodded off. The train moved on through the darkness past multiple neon signs, and then just before the Copiague station was announced a muffled sound came over the intercom. It sounded as if someone had said, "Discharge all passengers."

We exchanged anxious looks. "Is that what you heard?" The train came to a stop at Copiague.

The intercom crackled to life. "All passengers and crew, leave the train immediately." The same ominous message was continually repeated. The train door leading to the platform would not open. Finally, at the other end of the car, a man shouted that the door was opening at his end of the car. We awakened several young men who were stretched out on seats fast asleep as we headed for the open door.

It was a bomb scare. Passengers milled around on the platform. One conductor was banging on a train window. He was loudly telling another conductor to leave immediately.

Somehow our group got separated. Two of us assumed that if a bomb went off on the train, the platform was not the place to be. Halfway down the stairs we turned to look for the other two. We could not see Theresa DelToro. I ran back up the stairs. She was being casual. She wanted to find out more about what was going on. I screamed, "For God's sake, come down. This is a bomb scare!"

Finally, we were all at the bottom of the stairs. We ran to try to get the one cab in sight. It already had two male passengers. Before we could talk the driver into squashing us into his cab, a third man jumped into the backseat. We spied another cab several hundred feet away. Two of us in two-inch heels sprinted to be the first to get to the cab. Once we were all inside, we loudly talked at once. "Get us out in a hurry. There is the possibility of a bomb going off on the train."

The driver mistook the word "bomb" for "bum" and assured us, "You're okay now. You're inside my locked cab and safe with me." When he finally realized we were saying "bomb" instead of "bum," the gas pedal went to the floor. The cab jerked forward with tires squealing as he turned the corner to get away from what might be ground zero.

Since by now our curiosity was piqued when we got to Babylon, we just had to have the cab take us back to Copiague. Halfway there we couldn't see any light in the sky indicating excitement. We all went home.

When one member of our party described these events to her husband at what was now after four in the morning, his response was "Sure, now tell me what really happened."

Grandson Randy Santmann at the foot of Ayers Rock in Australia, 1998.

Granddaughter Katie feeding a kangaroo at a kangaroo farm in Australia, 1998.

Chapter 30

Road to Adelaide, Australia

This was going to be a wonderful adventure. I was taking two of my grandchildren, Randy and Katie, to the other side of the world.

It was July 24, 1998, and we were in Australia. It was as if a country so very new to Western civilization, two hundred years, had presented itself in such an unexpected way. Our jaded New York City eyes gratefully acknowledged clean streets, as well as friendly people. Such a recent newcomer to the modern world as we know it, and yet here it was only two hundred years after tens of thousands of years of exclusive aboriginal habitation, with its up-to-date buildings and latest technology. Never mind that the first European settlers came in English prison ships with a contingent of military personnel to keep them in check. Their landing place was Sydney, where an architect who had been put in prison for forgery designed many of the beautiful buildings in the city despite the area having a desolate, rocky terrain. Here were prisoners, many of whom were convicted of what today would be considered a minimum petty infraction, such as stealing a loaf of bread to feed a hungry family. From this beginning rose a proud city with buildings constructed from local materials—marble, limestone, and rocks on the rust-colored earth.

Sydney was ready to spread its wings for the 2000 Olympics. Would it rise above the huge amounts of money needed for large arenas, intricate transportation improvements, housing, etc.?

Melbourne, farther south, stood in a huff. It had an arena for over one hundred thousand people within its city limits, as well as a sophisticated transportation system and hostelry to accommodate many tens of thousands of tourists who were expected to be drawn to the Olympics.

The Australian people were a proud people with a culture very similar to that of the United States. They were privy to all of the same problems we faced on a daily basis—drugs, need for gun control, ever-expanding health-care costs, etc. At the same time, they were blessed, in a very similar manner to the people in the United States, with one of the highest standards of living in the world.

Australia had a total land mass of approximately the same size as that of the continental United States.

The coastal regions contained most of the population. Sydney had 4.5 million residents. Melbourne had almost four million, and Adelaide had one million people in a country with a total population of slightly over eighteen million, of which only 2 percent were aboriginal.

The aborigines lived mostly in the 70 percent central arid landmass, referred to as the bush or the outback, where rainfall averaged between none to ten inches a year. There were artesian aquifers, which raised questions. Where were they? How far down into the earth were they located? Was the water of a quality that was fit for human consumption? How long would they last? Could someone settle in the region and make a living where the aboriginal culture was such that a penalty for transgressions against society was a choice between modern law and the aboriginal spear in the leg?

Tourists seem to relate to Australia through their animal kingdom based on a visual imagination of koala bears (not friendly), kangaroos (friendly), and emus.

Melbourne and Sydney were raising the sophistication level of all of Australia, despite the fact that there were over five million sheep in Australia. The newborn sheep were called lambs, and the older sheep were called mutton. A few years ago, there was no market for sheep, and sheep were shot and buried by the thousands. Lambs at one time sold for ten cents each until the price rose to twenty-five cents.

Wool was stockpiled to over five million pounds by a farmer organization waiting for a market. The government was unhappy with the lack of a taxing entity, and the stockpile now stood at a little over one million. The world market had bottomed out. Russia, when the wall came down, ordered no more wool. They had been ordering a low grade. Japan, currently in bad straits, was ordering no more wool. Japan had been ordering a high grade for the fine wool suit market. All Australians were very concerned about the jittery state of the economy in Japan, where money had been flowing freely. Now they seemed at a loss as to how to approach a lowered standard of living.

Chapter 31

Wearing Out of Angel Wings

I had believed for many years that there was a little angel residing on my left shoulder, except on a short Florida vacation. It was as if my angel companion had taken a short vacation of its own.

It was January 4, 2001, and I was traveling to Florida from MacArthur Airport with a friend. There were no direct flights to Fort Lauderdale. We had finished our lunch during our two-hour layover at the Baltimore Washington Airport and were in line to board the last leg to our Florida destination. Horrors, I was having an episode of the trots. I made a frantic trip to the nearby women's room. I left my soiled underclothing in the women's room and cleaned up as best I could. Another episode happening on the plane was a constant threat for the rest of the flight. *Angel?*

On our way to my house in Florida, we were greeted with a cold snap of historical proportions. Turning on a breaker in the garage to start getting heat was of no consequence. The breaker kept popping back to the off position. *Call an electrician.* Not in ten years, but here it was in my hand: a dead phone. Where was my angel? It took over twenty-four hours but I finally got the best of all the current problems. On the last day of our stay, the weather was so balmy that a boat ride on the intercostal did not require a sweater.

On January 8, the 4:45 p.m. direct flight on Southwest from Fort Lauderdale back to MacArthur Airport had its own set of gremlins at work. We were on the plane, presumably ready for takeoff, when the dreaded words "We are having a mechanical problem. It is being checked, and we expect to be able to take off shortly" came over the sound system. Two hours later we were off that plane and on another one that had arrived from another destination. Finally, we were in the air and on our way to Long Island. The flight was uneventful.

It was nine o'clock, and the plane was in the final descent over MacArthur Airport. Looking outside in the plane's lights, I saw fat, wet snowflakes beating at us. Getting off the plane we were covered by a canopy. Then I got my one piece of checked luggage while I carried my purse in my small black carry-on.

It wasn't until I had picked up my luggage and left the building, heading in soft Italian loafers for the Islip resident parking lot, that I felt the full brunt of the nasty weather. A one-inch underfoot soup of syrupy cold slush quickly made its way through my fine footwear. The almost nonexistent lighting in the general direction of the Islip lot, along with the swirling falling snow, made visibility only several yards. I found myself in a parking lot with its many little Budget rental signs. By then it was impossible to see far enough to figure out the direction of the Islip lot. A man brushing off snow from his car windows, when I asked him if he knew where the lot was, informed me he was not familiar with the airport.

He offered to give me a ride to look for my car in the Islip lot. He looked like a legitimate fifty-year-old business man might look. I responded, "I know I shouldn't accept a ride, but you wouldn't rape me. It's too cold." He murmured a startled response about something from years before. I got in the car with my small suitcase on my lap and the keys to my car in my pocket. There were steamed windows in his car. He was fumbling with unfamiliar car controls as he scrunched down, trying to see in the two-inch clearance of frost at the bottom of the windshield. Skidding around, we finally saw a Budget car exit and then a one-way sign leading out of the lot.

Leaving the Budget lot, we saw the entrance to the Islip lot. Just inside and to the left, barely recognizable under its snow cover, was my beloved tan 1995 Acura Legend. I jumped out of the Budget car, suitcase and keys in hand, and merrily tossed over my shoulder to my knight in shining armor, "I love you." I pushed wet snow off my car windows and drove home, content and happy.

The garage door closed behind me. I went to reach for the small black carry-on, which contained my handbag, reading material, jewelry, etc. It wasn't on the backseat, nor was it on the front seat or in the trunk. No, that was not possible. My current life history was encompassed in its contents. There was a personal phone book, credit cards, my license and registration, cash from a recently cashed check, and a large diamond ring recently given to me by a very special friend. All of the bag's contents were in a stranger's car going to an unidentified location. I dashed to the answering machine in the house. There were twelve messages but not one from my mystery man. By now it was a little after ten o'clock.

The only thing left to do that gave me even a tiny glimmer of hope was to go back to the airport. When I reached the airport, I circled the parking area and then checked my prior Islip parking spot, which revealed nothing. I circled again to the front of the main building, which had nobody outside and very few people inside. It was now ten thirty. There were several young women and men behind the Budget rental desk. I was before them terribly embarrassed and frantic. My drawn facial expression, along with my explanation of the outrageous set of circumstances, with just a few dollars in my jeans pockets, seemed to trigger an outpouring of working concern.

They asked for the time of the incident. I answered, "Nine thirty p.m." They asked for the color of the car. "I think dark. It was mostly covered with snow." They asked if I remembered the numbers on the license plate. "No." They asked if it was a two-door or a four-door car. "I think it was a two-door car." And lastly they asked for the man's age and physical description. "About fifty, gray hair, medium height and build." Using their questions and my answers, the clerks at the Budget counter carefully went over their lists of people renting cars. The speculation of who it might be as they went up and down the lists had me praying even more frantically. It seemed as if they were not going to be able to locate the person for whom I was looking. Finally, after many maybes or outright nos, they settled on someone. The man was registered at the Holiday Inn off Nesconset Highway and Route 347. They called him, but there was no answer.

After more speculation, they decided to call the hotel lobby. A hotel clerk said a man had left a black bag with them. A woman he had given a ride to at the airport had left it in his car. The car he had registered in his name was a four-door gray car. I could not stop the sobs of relief. Soft murmured words of comfort drifted out from behind the Budget desk. The clerk gently laid out directions when I was finally able to talk. Through the many dark, icy miles from MacArthur Airport to the Holiday Inn desk, my angel and I had our quiet moments together. At the Holiday Inn I had a note slipped under the door of my knight in shining armor: "And now I know I love you." As a tiny token of my appreciation, I paid for his stay at the inn.

The next morning in the bookkeeping office, I was regaling the Little Flower Nursing Home staff with the rather outrageous set of circumstances of the previous night, with its angel finale. An employee from the front office came into the room with a smiling pixie look on her face. "I just got the strangest phone call. A man called from the Holiday Inn. He was fumbling for words and ended with 'Tell her I just can't accept.'"

I called the phone number he left, and he asked to take me out to dinner. I accepted and met him in a restaurant in Jamesport. Conversation flowed smoothly through dinner. He identified that he was an engineer working at Stony Brook Hospital on a project. There were no plans to meet again. The money I spent on the hotel room had been paid back.

After what seemed like so many situations where I'd identified to my office staff about my angel's gentle touch that seems to sway the end result of what might have had a negative outcome one of my employees piped up with "When you get to heaven there will be a row of angels with no wings because the wings will have been all worn out from working so hard for you." I assured her I really had only one that was my very own angel and that she too had her very own angel.

Chapter 32

Musing, Dad Samuel Patnode, and Others

I'm not sure I want to talk to you just now. It's 10:28 p.m. on Friday, February 2, 2001, and I just got back from having a very nice dinner at a nice Italian restaurant with a few friends.

Okay, I really don't think you have to explain to me. Well, maybe a little, and I'll try to understand.

I'll just start by telling you how I now look at what probably was your life. After your father and mother died and some of your brothers and sisters still lived at home, I think you may have assumed a supervisory role from the bits and pieces of family gossip that I've heard over the years. All of your siblings were basically smart, competitive, French-speaking, tall, and better-than-average-looking.

For eighteen years before you married my mother, you dated Katie White, who was a member of the Catholic Daughters of America. She was a schoolteacher who never left her mother to marry you. What did you do for those eighteen years between twenty-seven and forty-five, when you finally left Katie White and married my mother? Did you have a very special love, or was my mother after all of those eighteen years a fill-in because Katie White, the Catholic daughter, wouldn't leave her mother to marry you? You had to know that my mother was someone you could rely on to keep bringing your kids into the world as a very good Catholic.

Katie White had no brothers or sisters, and my mother had ten brothers and sisters, with four of them already in Saint Mary's in Pennsylvania. They were cloistered and holy, away from all manner of sin. After all, the days of nuns started in long prayers and ended the same way. That's not even counting the vows of poverty, the cloistered living in silence, except when praying out loud or teaching school or practicing nursing. They live in tiny rooms with Spartan furniture.

What did you and Katie White do during those eighteen years? I wanted to know, so on one of my trips to Saint Mary's, Pennsylvania, with other family members I asked Sister Paula if she knew of any intimate get-together between my father and Katie White. Other family members literally gasped in horror, but Sister Paula quietly answered that she did not know.

Two years ago a few of us Patnode kids started going on yearly summer pilgrimages to Saint Mary's to see whatever nuns were still living. As of last summer, Sister Jean Marie was the lone survivor of the four sisters who had joined the convent. During one of our visits Sister Jean Marie acknowledged that I was not only her godchild but also her only one. She repeated the fact several times and that she probably hadn't acknowledged me until these last few years because she was so very young when she became my godmother.

Somewhere in the reaches of my heart I try, but I'm not sure I'll ever forgive her for so many years of my waiting for her to acknowledge our special relationship. Somehow to many people being a godmother or godfather doesn't seem to matter very much. A godparent is supposed to be somebody very special to the child. After all, when they stand up by the often crying baby next to the water font in the church and holy water is being poured over the baby's head, the godparents promise to watch over the child's spiritual life if somehow the mother and/or the father cannot or will not.

I, Theresa, left my Ellenburg Center home, got married, and had two kids. They left home, got married, and had kids before Sister Jean Marie finally came forward to declare her godmother status. Could it possibly have anything to do with me acknowledging the relationship with gifts for her? Oh well, I can't really think about that too much. If I did maybe she'd stop saying all of those wonderful things about me after all of these years. She sure does say nice things.

I wonder what you would have been like if Katie White had married you. Would I be born? Would my brothers and sisters be born? What in heaven's name did you do and say to each other for those eighteen years?

I never had a chance to meet your mother and father. I don't know if I was even born before they died. My grandparents on your side spelled their name Patenaude. They lived through an epidemic. I don't know whether the people dying were both young and old. My Patnode grandparents lost several children who were, of course, your siblings. I remember being told of great family sadness when the kids died. Of course they weren't the only ones with dying children. Many families lost children. I don't remember you talking about this, but every once in a while your sister, Aunt Lillian, that wonderful woman who lived in Plattsburgh, New York, would let me in on a little family history. She was another one of those women, like Mrs. Smith, who I loved so much. Her house was very big. Her husband seemed sort of nonexistent. He almost never spoke and was so much in the background that it seemed almost as if he wasn't alive. Her daughter Ester and whatever the name of the other one was were both kind of snotty to us Patnode kids. They were a bit older and acted very stuck up.

One time, because of a snow storm, I stayed overnight with a friend of my sister Rose in Ellenburg Center, New York. The only reason that Rose and I weren't at our house and that Rose hadn't already gone back to Malone, New York, was the storm. Rose was a student with the nuns in Malone. With no money for Rose to have her room and board paid for at the convent school, Rose worked in the kitchen to cover the cost. She came home to Ellenburg Center once in a while. Well, anyway, for that one night in all of the years of my childhood, we ended up at that Ellenburg Center house. Actually, the girl living in that house wasn't really a friend of Rose; rather, she was trying out the Malone Catholic School.

I think that her mother and father were paying for her tuition from the beer hall they ran on the first floor. My brother would go to the beer hall. My parents did their best to keep him away from the very bad experience of all the drinking going on there, but they sure weren't very successful.

Their house was a mess. Sagging bed frames held up sagging mattresses. The most interesting thing about the second-floor living quarters was that one wall was covered from floor to ceiling with cardboard boxes. I expect that was because the whole family was squished into the rather small second-floor living quarters.

The day after my overnight stay in the second-floor living quarters in Ellenburg Center, I visited my aunt Stella in Plattsburgh and got a surprise. I was feeling very uncomfortable and itchy. On seeing one tiny moving thing on my skin and remembering how itchy I felt lying on the bed the night before, I realized, *Oh my God, I have bedbugs on me.* Aunt Stella didn't bat an eye as I sobbed and tore at my clothes. She calmly helped me undress and looked me over to see wherever else the little monsters might be nesting or moving. I got a bath, and she washed my clothes while speaking softly and calmly to me. She was such a love that even now years later thinking about her gives me a warm glow. I don't know if Rose carried any bedbugs back to the convent, but I guess I would have heard about it, though I don't know why it would have been only me that the bedbugs liked.

Then the most treasured memory of Aunt Stella was when I was ten or twelve years old. The popular article of clothing for girls was a crocheted triangle to wear as a headpiece. That wonderful precious aunt crocheted one for me. It had a white cream middle with the very softest blue-green edging. I loved her so. She never raised her voice, cooked wonderful meals, and never showed me anything but love, even though I rarely could get to Plattsburgh to see and visit this treasured woman. She had such a big heart for the whole world, and I was so very happy I seemed to fit into that world.

Chapter 33

Around the World

It was October 2001, and a pall of sadness hung over the John F. Kennedy Airport. Every person I met knew someone who was connected to the destruction of the twin towers on September 11, 2001. The airport that normally would be bustling was strangely almost empty. There were a few stragglers here and there. I had gotten to the airport over three hours early. I left Babylon at half past noon for a five o'clock flight to Seattle. I was alone at the check-in counter. The young lady behind the counter knew several of the stewardesses who were on the plane that hit the towers. I went on to the lounge of United Airlines. For over one hour I was the only person in the lounge. Finally, a young woman came into the lounge. She had a story about the carnage. She had been sitting in her friend's office, with its beautiful view of the World Trade Center. She watched as the second plane went crashing into the World Trade Center.

On the plane from JFK to Seattle, the young man sitting next to me had a grandmother who lived almost across the street from the World Trade Center. Her car was in a garage at the time of the attack. If it had been in front of her building, it would have been part of the destruction. Almost all of the people I met on this trip seemed to be affected in an almost vague way. It was eight thirty in the morning, and we were sitting in the Seattle airport waiting to board our private jet around the world. The one other person from the New York area

189

was reassuring someone on the phone that she loved them. I could overhear other conversations. There was talk of places where people had visited, operations for this or that, etc. All were so cheerful, while I was still reeling from the attack on the World Trade Center. Didn't they understand we may be going to war after such a terrible blow to our very being?

September 11 had started out with the usual morning ritual of turning on the radio while I was preparing to go to work as the administrator of the Little Flower Nursing Home. Something sounded different from the usual broadcast, so I turned on the television. It was as if what I was seeing couldn't possibly be occurring. The first tower of the World Trade Center had been hit. I sat there and saw the second tower being hit. How could this be happening? I went to the village to cast a vote in a local election. The poles were closed. As I was crossing the street, a neighbor I knew well was passing by. With tears in my eyes I asked, "Have you heard about the World Trade Center?" She casually answered yes, looked at me rather strangely, and went on her way.

Soon nursing homes were alerted to expect patients from city hospitals in order to accept patients wounded by the World Trade Center attack. We scrambled in anticipation of an unknown number of patients coming from the city. Could we possibly get beds from the Red Cross or the Salvation Army, supplies from drugstores, extra linen and water supplies? Finally, word came back. There was no need. Most of the people in the World Trade Center were dead!

It was a quarter to ten, and we were sitting on the plane. I'd called the Little Flower Nursing Home, feeling a need to touch base with the reality of my life, its problems, and its everyday concerns that seemed to barely touch these world travelers. The plane was fitted to accommodate fewer passengers, allowing for luxurious seating. Champagne was passed out as we got on board and throughout the flight. All kinds of goodies were immediately laid out, including shrimp cocktail, assorted cheeses, etc.

Where did reality lie? We from the New York area expected the world to be changed forever with war that was being waged on our very shores. All of the scenes around me seemed almost obscene. The plane was filled with people who were laughing and talking about such mundane nothings as they moved in such a lap of luxury. We were never to be the same again, or were we? It was not even a month after 9/11"my God" is this what we are asked to do, to go on with our lives? I heard such words of fluff and saw the luxurious spending. Were most people to lead a light uninvolved life as we went on? Who were these people who seemed so unaffected? Was this our "me" society or our society of self-preservation? What did it all mean?

Am I abandoning the battlefield, what seems to lie in my current values? What are they? Was I going on to reclaim that which I may have lost, or was I part of a herd of a self-indulgent "me" generation? Was this the end product in its largesse, the result of the American dream? I almost wished I could abandon the questions that plagued me. Let those generations quickly closing on our heels be the bearers of the burdens so recently imposed by the shocking disaster. Would it be a call to arms or a call to mankind?

We were going down the runway. Planes were taking off. All I could think of was all that fuel in flames pouring down the elevator shafts, spreading on each floor, incinerating everyone and everything in its path, till one terrible burst of cataclysmic energy burned everything in sight. *Please, God, spare someone.* But even those outside were hit with glass and debris. Some lived. Some died.

I didn't even know the time and date. Here we were, a chattering group of terribly indulged people. Outside the plane windows puffy white clouds of various shapes and sizes sometimes hid the washboard ocean below. It was almost as if the farther we got from ground zero, the awful rending of the very fabric of life seemed to be distancing in every way with the miles. Was I happy or sad over starting to feel less tearful, less wrenched with sadness? After all, this trip was around the world. Was this part of life, or was it an escape that didn't deserve to be?

For many miles I felt bereft of the family, such as my children and grandchildren, with whom I had traveled in the past. It was going on for over two years, the miniscule touches with my daughter as the administrator of the Petite Fleur Nursing Home, which is done in such a clinical fashion that only adds to the anguish. How could someone who I loved so dearly, such as is demonstrated with a blanket on the snow on a cold winter night? Her admonition of "If I'm cold I'm going into the house" kept me moving gingerly if a hand or ear or whatever got exposed to the cold with a quick scramble to cover whatever part of her body might be feeling the cold. The sky was filled with an exquisite display of dark blue and sparkling stars which seemed to cover our universe. My guardian angel let me smile through my tears.

In Seattle I was so sure I had lost a diamond ring that I liked and wore every day. I felt so badly. The beginning of the trip was such a loss, far beyond the value of the ring. Every paranoid ideology developed. Was it the maid? I took my $10 tip back. I searched the suitcase and the carry-on. I had started to resign myself to the inevitable of a stolen ring that would possibly taint the rest of the trip. In one last effort I moved things on the nightstand—the phone, the lamp—and there it was. I knew it was my angel once again.

What an incredible feeling of relief at having been blessed. Now the horizon stretched out in a singular white haze over which was a solid pale-blue sky. Below the white haze was the never-ending stretch of the blue washboard ocean. Peace started to descend over my troubled soul, reassuring me that life is what I make it. Life circled around.

Chapter 34

Amboseli National Park, Africa

The very most that anyone could hope for in life was to have experiences that surpassed what might be perceived as beyond your greatest expectations.

It was the fifth day of a Micato Safari, where the terrain, accommodations, natives, and incidents far outperformed anything I could have imagined. I was in the Amboseli National Park at the Ol Tukai Lodge. The hotel cottages formed a compound ringed by an electric fence. The electric fence kept the elephants out. They loved the bark. Their voracious appetite spelled death to the trees. Bark was nature's way of nourishing trees, as well as providing protection from various insects and animals. I was on a small platform in front of my attached cottage, where I was comfortably seated in one of the two chairs. Nearby trees were of a majestic height, stretching their feathery green foliage into a pale-blue sky, with its various patches of big and small fluffy white clouds. A truck rumbled past with three natives. It was pulling an empty flatbed trailer. A baboon was taking a stroll. Its impressive face casually glanced in my direction. Five inches of its tail were in a rigid upright position, with the balance hanging limply. Its greenish-brown fur blended beautifully into the greenish-brown landscape. Majestic Kilimanjaro, Africa's highest mountain at 19,340 feet, stood like a sentinel in the distant horizon as its white snow-covered peak added to its quiet grandeur.

A native of small stature wrapped in a flowing red garment from shoulder to ankles wearing sandal and carrying a five-foot-long stick was hurrying past. He crossed over the four-wire electrified fence held upright by three various-sized poles that were about three to five feet in height and spaced about seventy feet apart. What was he doing? After crossing to the other side of the fence, he seemed to be running with or after a baboon. They kept running, as I kept spying on them. I knew that hunting was prohibited in this area. Soon the two were so distant that without spyglasses they were dark specks against the distant forest line. It looked as if he was still many feet from the running baboon, and he raised his stick as if to throw. Finally, he stopped and started to walk back at a leisurely pace. He crossed the fence, glanced over at me, and walked past.

Later I learned that in one of the nearby cottages a woman was sleeping. She had left her purse on a little table next to a screened window. A baboon walking past tore open the screen and started to explore the contents. Pill bottles with their colorful contents made the biggest hit. The baboon opened the bottles and popped the contents into his mouth. The woman awoke and in her state of awareness assumed she was dreaming and went back to sleep. A bit later, again awake, she found herself face-to-face with the baboon. For a moment she thought that the baboon was a reincarnation of her husband. Her screams brought a rescue.

The red-garmented native who I had seen had been sent to chase the baboon and try to hit it to discourage baboons from visiting the compound. Being too tired to continue, he had finally given up the chase. I asked what would be done about the woman's missing medications. The answer was that the closest hospital would be contacted and enough replacement medication would be secured to get her home.

Grandson Randy with grandmother Theresa, who is holding the Russian guard's shotgun as he stands beside her. When passengers are allowed to leave the ship to stand on solid ice, Russian guards accompany with a shotgun at the ready in case any polar bears might be in the vicinity, July 2004.

A picture of the ship Yamal as taken from the ship's helicopter, July 2004.

Randy and his grandmother standing next to the Yamal at the site of the North Pole as determined by the ship's crew, July 2004.

Chapter 35

Yamal
(Nuclear-Powered Russian Icebreaker)

It was July 1, 2004, and my grandson Randy Santmann and I were going on a trip to the North Pole on the *Yamal*. The *Yamal's* statistics were very impressive. There were two nuclear reactors that provided steam for propulsion and were encased in 160 tons of steel. It had 75,000 total horsepower, or 55.3 MV, enough horsepower to supply a town of 18,750 homes. It had an armor steel icebreaker hull 48 mm thick.

Grandson Randy with grandmother Theresa wearing life jackets aboard the nuclear powered Russia icebreaker the Yamal in preparation for a helicopter ride off the ship, July 2004.

The troublesome details never stopped. I must apply to Quark expedition to go to the North Pole and then try to get Randy his passport. I had sent monies for the trip with an assumption that the airline tickets were being ordered by Quark when they hadn't been.

After I got the passports in order, with both of us sending for visas to be allowed into the Russian port to board the *Yamal*, I called Randy. The trip was to start Thursday July 1, 2004. I was talking to Randy on Sunday, June 27, 2004, about something to do with the trip, and he casually asked me if I had my Russian visa and passport. I had received mine a week earlier. He had not received his. I frantically called the visa company early Monday morning. I had called a week earlier and was told they had just arrived from the Russian Embassy and that they would be sent out the next day. The package finally came on June 29.

On August 1 the trip started from John F. Kennedy Airport to Helsinki, Finland. The city was such a neat and tidy place with pleasant and accommodating people. The next morning the people who were going on the *Yamal*, all seemingly speaking languages other than English, were milling about. Suitcases of the people who were going to the ship were scattered about. I had a rather large suitcase. After all, this was going to be a long trip. Finally, a woman became the obvious leader of the group. She was checking suitcases. When she got to mine, she said I would not be allowed to board the *Yamal* with that size of suitcase. There were only a few minutes left before a bus was coming for the group. The one suitcase was all the luggage I had with me. I frantically asked what might be done. She spoke the native tongue and found out there was a luggage store around the block. We ran to the store, where I was able to get a much smaller suitcase, and then ran back to the hotel. I quickly packed as much as I could into the new suitcase. I was assured that my large suitcase would be waiting for me when I returned. By that time it was as if that surely was of little consequence one way or the other. There was a surreal quality to this trip, with its twenty-four hours of daylight. We were the only Americans. Passengers came from all parts of the world speaking indistinguishable languages. Randy was much younger than anyone else on board. I tried to make his trip as pleasant as I could by not asking him to eat with me at every meal, not keeping the same daytime and nighttime hours, etc. At first he seemed to be rather isolated, until the passengers somehow located his talent for manipulating picture taking—for example, making the American flag appear in back of someone at the North Pole. Randy spent much time in the small ship's library.

The ship's helicopter added a great deal to the enjoyment by flying us to small islands we would be passing. At every stop we were not allowed on land until a Russian guide went onshore ahead of us. They were dressed in heavy yellow slickers and carried shotguns in order to make sure we were not going to unexpectedly run into polar bears. They allowed us to hold the shotguns while standing next to them for photo ops.

It was nighttime and I was catching one fleeting moment. I was back on the forty-foot *Wicky One*. She was the yacht I had in my backyard for years. I loved her so. The hint of tears sprang to my eyes. The cabin that Randy and I had on the *Yamal* had the same feel. It was the only one on the *Yamal* that had such luxury. The bedroom had a full-size bed and its own porthole, like the *Wicky* had. The slight vibration under its ample size, with the muffled sound of the throbbing motor, was the result of the lapping waves against the *Wicky's* hull in the dead of night. Even its ample storage and head with a shower and tub more than met the *Wicky's* opulence.

Randy's stateroom had a sleeper sofa, a desk, a television, and walk-around space. Two portholes overlooked a passing sea of gently rising waves intermittently interrupted by a small white splash while our great ship surged ahead.

It was five in the morning, and the light of day had been streaming through the portholes for hours. I found endless pleasure in sitting on the small shelf below the porthole in Randy's stateroom, watching an endless array of huge chunks of ice being thrown aside in white cascades of water by the *Yamal*. The sounds were a reminder of an era of my life with love for the sea and love of the closeness of family. What a pleasure.

The powerful *Yamal* crunched through the ice day and night with ceaseless energy. Sometimes when the ice was too compact, with no long slivers of open water anywhere on the horizon, the low growl of the motors would lessen and the shuddering of the ship would become less intense until the ship stopped. The ship had hit ice so thick that it could not continue going forward. It was then put in reverse for a half mile or so and then once again plowed forward. Sometimes this happened several times more. If forward motion could not be attained, the reverse course was continued and another route was chosen.

The rules of the sea were that if a ship was caught in the ice and an icebreaker was within motoring distance, the icebreaker must go to the rescue even if that meant that the trip to the North Pole could not be completed. There were strict time guidelines for getting back to home port. Such an incident was reported to have happened. The people on board got so disruptive that the ship's captain proceeded to have a special landing on an island while returning to home port.

To *Yamal*, the Mama Bear of the Sea

At first you disturbed me with the endless crunching of huge ice flowing against your hull. Sometimes you stopped and retreated and then moved forward again. Mostly you went forward as the huge ice relentlessly ground against you—in reverse a bit too much for comfort and then forward again. You were a true warrior of the north—now forward again as the pitch of crunching ice rose, and then all stopped again. There was a bleak horizon of blue and white. Reverse to back up again. This time the reverse movement was more intense—back, back, back. Water churned from our sides in a white froth, and then you moved forward again, forming huge chunks of breaking ice along your side. Slowly you came to a stop again. The third try and still no success. On the fourth try at 2:00 a.m., you moved into reverse again with no success. After this reverse you found another route in order to keep moving on toward the North Pole.
The breaks in the horizon went on and on. Daylight never ended across the expanse of patches of blue ice among fields of white snow.

You felt as part of my body and spirit. You would not be stopped. The terrain was as one. It said you would not, you could not. My stubborn defense would not be thwarted by your exclusive identity and defy all intruders to my world, to my beauty, to my splendor on huge ethereal stages of heaping mountains of ice and snow as you wend your puny advances on my singular, as well as mammoth, floating icebergs.

You demanded her way. I was of nuclear strength. You could not and would not stop me. Maybe.

You moved huge hunks of ice measuring twenty, thirty, one hundred feet across. Looking out over the water I could see blue frozen ice rising to ten-foot-high ridges of snow with five or more feet of blue ice forming its base.

The theater of ever-moving sea, snow, and ice rose in your powerful thrust. Did you not tire? Your power against this unforgiving beautiful wasteland was challenging the unforgiving, endless sea of dark crevasse while splintering mammoth ice flowed.

In my heart, you were mine, this great protective being challenging the fiercest elements that the earth projected. Was there a time when you might waver?

No! You were mine and you would forever be in my dreams. There you were, and you would remain invisible. I loved you. Moving great sheets of ice, you were my queen. How could you challenge the unchallengeable? It had to do with your heart and soul and the beautiful mastery of a challenge never answered.

We were so close to the North Pole. There were still gaps here and there in the huge ice flows with dark blue to black spaces between the ice. As the Yamal thrusts she often closes over the dark spaces with ice flows being pushed across the dark water to join the other flows sometimes creating wedged upheaval of small mountains.

Chapter 36

The Little Flower Residence: Rescinding Operating Certificate

The sixty-nine-bed Little Flower Residence had become such a drag with seemingly endless violations from the New York State Health Department, on everything from medication deliveries to housekeeping, sizes of rooms, etc. An inspection done on December 26 and 27, 2004, resulted in a June 2005 report of thirty pages of violations, from counted flies in a light fixture to the percent of rust on floor radiators. I had till July 7, 2005, to make all of the corrections before fines would be imposed. The rate being paid for a resident in an adult home was twenty-nine dollars a day, which made building improvements, as well as hiring more employees, impossible. At some time in the previous year I was told by a government employee that I could not close the residence because it was the residents' home. Running in the red for two years finally came to a close on June 30, 2005. The New York State Health Department, as well as several other people representing government entities, when they had been notified of the expected closing date, were at the Little Flower Residence for several days before June 30 to make sure the letter of the law was being followed.

On June 29 I received a call at the Little Flower Nursing Home from Nancy, the administrator of the Little Flower Residence. A woman from the New York State Health Department wanted to talk to me. Nancy was having a hard time placing two residents in another licensed facility. One was a problematic drunk, and the other was a slovenly, nasty woman. There were extensive demands that were mandated by the health department before an adult home or a nursing home was given permission to close. Each resident to be moved must approve by sight and interview the accepting facility. The last two residents had refused every proposal.

First, I was told to admit them as patients to the Little Flower Nursing Home. Next, a man from the health department got on the phone. The conversation went on for at least twenty minutes. He said, "You can't close. You put in writing that you would make sure everyone was placed before closure." Then came threats. "McManus was fined $38,000. I wouldn't want anything to happen to you by putting your violations in writing." He ended the conversation with "I'll call you back later today."

I would not promise to stay open, because I had already made a deal with another licensed adult home that the health department had forbidden anyone be sent to. I had already made arrangements for the last two residence to be picked up at the Little Flower Residence on June 30.

I had prepared a closure letter for the New York State Health Department, with dates left open. The morning of June 30 I called the Little Flower Residence. Nancy was not at the residence. The same people from the June 29 New York State Health Department visit were at the residence, along with several other officious types. Nancy was making a last-ditch effort to make the last placement, that of the slovenly woman to a Nassau adult home. The woman and all of her belongings had been put in the residence station wagon. The time between Nancy departing with the resident, the health department at the residence, the uncertainty of whether the resident would accept the adult home she was being taken to, and Nancy returning to take charge of the building was very stressful indeed.

Even though there were no residents left in the building when the health department people arrived on June 30, they went into the office. An employee named Sheila, who was in charge, followed them into the office. They started looking things over on Nancy's desk and tried to open a locked drawer. The man asked Sheila for the patient fund book, to which she didn't have access. They left for lunch and told Sheila they would be back.

I was making frequent calls to the residence. When I heard they were coming back, I called a lawyer. The next step was to fax a signed closure letter with a June 30, 2005, noon closure time to be given to the inspectors on their return from lunch. Sheila showed them the letter, which they said they didn't need. Nancy returned. They asked her only a couple of questions and then took the copies of the adult home license and the medication delivery license off the wall and said, "You're no longer in business," and left.

Chapter 37

Memories

Flames great bursting sheets enveloping, swallowing, smoke choking dense. Years of work, lives spent in building, fixing over, going up in fire. No more horse to gallop in front of the barn and daringly sweep in the carriage house. No more jumping in the hay or fighting of the kids on the beams. All going up in smoke. No more going on trips with the horse and dog; the dog burnt. Think of it, hair smelling; a howling dog dying with his hair smoking, his flesh curling. No more trips where he chases chipmunks, where he follows, barks at me and my horse enjoying himself as I am.

Great red sheets of flaming timbers standing on end. Beams with nails still protruding lying about, smoldering red and threatening. Cement steps where we used to play trying to keep our balance now covered with flaming beams and great red sheets of tin.

Lots of machinery was saved you say. Oh yes! But what of the memories incased in the dear old frame that can never be rebuilt or replaced. Dreams lost and buried beneath the ashes of flaming tons of hay. Hay and grain men sweated and worked many days and weeks over. Things it takes a man many years to regain and no matter how many years pass is never made up in lost memories hopes and nameless little treasures.

Remember sleeping in the hay loft shortly before the fire, a great adventure. Playing hide and seek in the depths of the newly drawn hay. Seeing the barn being filled with a fork and motor I saw the hands of my father put up.

Do you remember the chickens I went and got down in the well; I had to get a ladder to be able to get down the well to reach them? The many chickens that fell down the small drain and Dad let me get it because it took a small hand to reach down far enough to get the little chicks. Now all filled with ashes.

The calf I tried to pull out of the hay mow bellowing as I was crying because it was so hard and I doubted my ability to do so. I covered it when it rained and loved it when the sun shone.

There was a ladder which consisted of a few boards nailed across from one beam to the next that went to the top of the barn. Remember the many times we used to run up the shaky stairs to the top where there was an excellent view of the surrounding countryside? In the old section in the back of the barn where one shaky plank was the only thing that reached from one side to another and was many feet over cement but now there is nothing to show for it.

The grain we used to bury each other in is still smoking on the third day of the disaster. Climbing to the very top of the middle part of the west section to jump into the part filled with straw and sometimes jumping into its soft depth afraid I might hit the middle beam but never doing so, now it's burned. Making a small opening from the middle of the barn where hay was stored to where the straw was stored in another part of the barn by slowly digging and crawling through the hay. The slight panicky feeling when I got stuck and had to get helped by encouragement or scolding from behind to move. Remember helping to throw down the hay thru a hole in the floor for feeding the animals or playing on its far spreading floor when it was empty of hay. Remember dragging the small sled out of the barn, hitching the horse and driving over the snow banks trying to tip the occupants of the small sleds that were tied to my bigger sled. My numb fingers but happy face when I came back and tried to unhitch the horse making slow but steady progress doing so. Happy memories gone.

No more feeding the horse grain after a tiring ride over the abundant land. No more hills to climb over hunting for the cows, getting angry when I found them hidden very securely in a small bunch in a corner of the forest but really feeling pleased with myself at having been able to find them. Letting the cows run way ahead then galloping quickly letting the wind whip my hair back as I caught up with them once more. I tried to make the dog leave the cows alone so they wouldn't get exhausted for milking. I reached the brook and let my tired horse drink. The panting dog was lapping at the clear cold water in which I let the horse stand.

One day the dog attacked a porcupine, biting, shaking it, getting filled with its cruel quills but not caring as long as he won and killed this threatening animal confronting himself and his master.

Riding the horse on long rides at times for pleasure, sometimes to hunt for lost animals, to pick berries, to deliver messages, now all impossible to do. The horse I trained to walk with me while on its back so I could open the gate at the pasture's entrance and then the sliding door to the barn to allow the cows to enter. Filling the salt trough and then watching the cows enjoy licking at it, the horses slipping out to get their licks, was work with pleasure.

The cow my brother couldn't control and when I went over to it quieted down and didn't kick any more. The heifers I helped to drive down from the upper pasture in freezing weather, wild and bellowing all the way until finally being driven into the warm barn that is now a heap of useless ashes. The time a cow had a new calf, me and my sister carried it down from the mysterious forest over rocky hilly countryside with a bellowing mother right on our heels. My brother came along and made us put it down. He drove it the rest of the way home after we had carried it over the most difficult parts.

Remember the rare dainty ferns with the black stems I found and carried on the horse. They were almost all wilted and the dirt had been all shaken out by the time I got to the neighbor who I was bringing them to. The excitement of finding the rare jack-in-the-pulpit. The frightening sensation of having a partridge suddenly flying out of undercover and startling my horse. The time I carried twelve partridge eggs on horseback from the forest to the barn only to set a hen on the nest and have her leave before the eggs were hatched.

I so wanted them to hatch and was so disappointed. Dad had told me that the chicks would be about the size of a bumble bee when they were born. Once my horse stepped on a nest of half-grown ones. Watching them half fly and run to escape was exciting.

Sometimes for fun in early spring we went in the forest at night to boil sap to make maple syrup. Dad would tell stories. The dog was sitting by my side. The fire was crackling and making many shadows in the darkening forest while keeping us warm from the cold wind. Remember gathering sap from the maple trees in the forest on a horse-drawn sled. The horses trudging from one tree to another.

Sliding down the big hill behind the team of horses and dragging our feet so not to run under the sled taking a chance of breaking our necks while our father wasn't looking. One time sliding down the hill alone I hit a stump and all the buttons of my jacket popped off ending in a bloody nose and my child-size boots.

Remember trying to get a Christmas tree with an older brother and sisters and the ice water went up over my child size boots. I had to go back to the house. I cried all the way because I couldn't go up in the woods with my brother and sisters.

THE END

The original writing that I sent to my aunt Stella was mailed back to me by her husband, Fred Maggini, after Stella's death, with a note dated May 12, 1980, that read,

> Theresa,
> Please do not destroy these memories of yours. Pat (Estella)
> cherished the enclosed very much, so did I. Please keep it
> & pass it on to the kids.
>
> Fred M.

Chapter 38

A Life Filled With Wonderful Memories

Theresa and granddaughter Katie, August 1989.

4/29/88 Theresa M. Santmann at work at Little Flower Nursing Home with granddaughter Katie on her desk

Grandchild Katie with four new teeth in a playpen in Grandma Santmann's Little Flower Nursing Home Office, October 29, 1988.

Theresa's granddaughter Catherine advancing her love of horses
with her grandmother at their Florida getaway, 1991.

*Theresa visiting a goat farm
near Rouses Point, New York. She is holding
the baby goat that she will be bringing home
in a large cardboard box with hay in
the bottom that will be fastened by a
seat belt, June 1988.*

*Theresa
holding her
baby goat
while her son-
in-law David
Grossman holds
his daughter
Katie, Theresa's
granddaughter,
June 26, 1988.*

*Katie on one of her first
horseback riding lessons with
her grandmother Theresa
on their visit to
her home in Boca Raton,
Florida, January 1991.*

Theresa at her Little Flower Nursing desk holding grandson Randy while feeding granddaughter Katie, June 1, 1988.

Theresa giving a bottle feeding to grandchild Mathew at her desk at the Little Flower Nursing Home, April 10, 1992.

Grandchildren Randy and Katie enjoyed playing together.

Grandchildren Katie and Randy tiptoeing into the ocean at a Boca Raton, Florida beach, 1989.

Granddaughter Katie at Lion Country Safari in Florida, September, 1991.

Theresa delivering pregnant cows to farmers hard hit by an ice storm in northern New York State, 1998.

Grandchildren Randy, Katie, and Mathew taking a break during a horseback riding jaunt in upstate New York, 1999.

The members of the Babylon Village Youth Project posing in front of their clubhouse called Santmann House. Grandchildren Mathew and Katie are standing in front of the group on the right-hand side of the picture, 1996.

Theresa with grandchildren Randy and Katie next to the Alaska pipline in year of 1997. It was built in 1977 at a cost of eight billion dollars to move oil. It is 800 miles long and accounts for 25 percent of US oil.

Grandchildren Randy and Katie on a visit to Alaska.

Theresa front right with black hat, granddaughter Katie red hat in front, 1997.

*Grandchildren
Randy
and Katie
enjoying a
helicopter
ride in
Alaska, 1997.*

*Grandchildren
Randy and Katie
with their
grandmother,
who were
helicoptered to the
top of the iceberg
when traveling in
Alaska, 1997.*

*Theresa making her
first and last international trip
with her three grandchildren
Randy, Katie, and Mathew to
Zermatt, Switzerland, 1999.*

*Theresa traveling
in Kenya, visiting with African
school children in Laikipia,
South Africa, October 2005.*

Grandson Randy having his picture drawn in Rome, Italy, while his grandmother Theresa looks on August 24, 2003.

Randy and Theresa in Rome Italy, August 24, 2003.

Entrance of Russian Nikita Khrushchev underground shelter ten stories below ground in Moscow, Russia. It was to be utilized if needed during the 1962 Cold War with the United States.

Theresa having her picture taken with a Russian cosmonaut who has been to the Russian space station several times, April 2008.

Theresa posing inside an actual Russian space suit.

The bottom of the space capsule being railroaded from the area where it was built to its destination for launching. Both Russian and Korean cosmonauts were to be on board, April 2008.

Theresa having her picture taken with the first woman in space, Soviet cosmonaut Valentina Tereshkova, April 2008. On June 16, 1963 Valentina achieved 48 orbits and 71 hours in space and then returned to earth.

Theresa's brother Ray Patnode as a sailor based aboard the U. S. S. Telepon, July 1960.

Brother of Theresa Patnode, Raymond Patnode, giving his nephew John Santmann a ride at the Patnode Fort Jackson, New York, farm.

Chapter 39

Odds and Ends

The following is a letter from brother Ray:

U.S.S. *Telepon*
July 7, 1960

Dear Theresa,

We'll be going out to sea again on the 12th so thought I would write while I have the chance. I had planned on going home sometime near Christmas but it's still too early to know. If I get a swap I'll be in Japan at the time but I rather doubt it as I would have to put in for it by the 12th and I don't think the division officer will approve it. I'll have to settle for a one week trip to Alaska.

I'm glad you like your new place. I don't think I would care for city living, especially with a family. What a name for a dog. I think Bum is much easier to remember.

I often think of Dad but every time I do my thoughts become more mixed up. It seems that in the back of my mind I think of him as he must have been on the first farm although I can hardly remember. It seems he was big, strong and always sure of himself. We didn't have much time to listen to our hard luck stories but most of us respected him for all that. After the barn burned or I should say while the barn was still burning he was making plans for rebuilding and no one knew or even thought about the actual effect this would have on him. I don't think he even really wanted to move although he knew it was best. After that as the years went by he saw more and more of his ideas being rejected, so to speak. Not used to having his ideas questioned he became bitter and after a while, thought it was our stubbornness which made us do everything just the opposite of what he wanted which was, to a great extent true for both sides. As he grew older and after his heart attack we did most of the work which meant we did it just about the way we wanted to unless his way was better. By this time he was so set in his way that no one else was ever right and not being able to work after always working hard all his life made him restless which made it hard for him to sleep at night. This naturally put him in a bad mood the next day and though everyone has their bad days he was becoming that way all the time. After a while he started wanting sympathy which was very much against his nature to ask for although he did come to do so many, many times. After that he started envying other people whom he thought got more attention or more sympathy. After he got to this point it was only a matter of time. I haven't much doubt that his death was caused more by his mental condition than his physical condition. It makes me shiver to think of him as I last saw him. He was so pale, his skin was cold and he looked like a living skeleton. I felt almost sick and thought about how much he had suffered. I wonder if it could have been avoided and can't help but think that someway he could still be living a full happy life and the circumstances which caused him to live the last ten years in misery, could somehow have been avoided.

I guess all that doesn't make much sense but it's just the mood I'm in that makes me write like that.

About copying your letter, that was the first time I have ever done it and then only because I didn't have time to write a letter before we left for picket but still I apologize and promise I won't do it again. I guess I've written a lot without writing anything but since there is nothing to write will close for now.

Love, Ray

Theresa Santmann as a student at Farmingdale College year 1968

Instructor's note on submitted writing assignment

"A delightful expose of the conspiracy. I didn't realize you were so adept at double entendre"

If the people of the United States would only open their eyes they would realize that communism is everywhere on the verge of taking over the world. The schools are on the focal point of all communist doctrine. What better way to take over a country than through the unsuspecting and easily influenced young. My mother felt very strongly that this was the situation but I wasn't so sure. I liked most of my teachers and the principal. When you like someone it's hard to believe that that knowingly or unknowingly he or she is taking part in a monstrous plot.

My mother believed that communist trickery was evident everywhere. Her proof of this was how little the parents had to say about some of the things they were doing with us kids in school. A good example of this was the school authorities making us expose our bodies. Any baring of the body was demeaning and made us more susceptible to communist doctrine.

By the time I reached the seventh grade I had to attend a large central school. In this school we were subjected to a physical once a year by a medical doctor. Imagine, all the girls were made to strip to the waist and then given a little diaper like cloth to cover their breasts. It sure didn't cover very much. Of coarse any one with any decency found this very repugnant. It was a perfect way to get one to subjugate her will to a foreign doctrine. My mother sure let the principal know about this.

Take the case of the showers after gym. There was one main shower for all those hussies who brazenly showered together in groups of five or six. They had already given in to the foreign doctrine. After all it isn't natural to be willing to let just anybody see you in the nude. There were two private showers for those of us with more decency. Even so in the rush to get out of the locker room there would be a bare torso and that was just too much. My mother probably had more to say to the principal than any other parent in the school district. No wonder.

Another example was all those cheerleaders jumping around during the basketball games. They were a disgrace. You could see there legs up to their panties. They were a disgrace; and in front of all those people. Who but my mother would have suspected those sneaky reds under these circumstances? It only stood to reason that girls wouldn't be delighted to show off their bodies unless they were encouraged to do so by the school authorities.

I didn't get very upset about the medical examinations. The showers were not a traumatic experience and I loved being a cheerleader so my mother suspected I might be a bit of a hussy and hopefully nothing worse.

If it wasn't for Father Coughlin and his weekly newspaper my mother would have been in pickle trying to keep abreast of the current communist tactics. As it was she did manage to keep me from becoming pink. It was a hard fight.

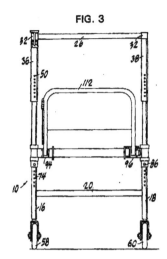

FIG. 3

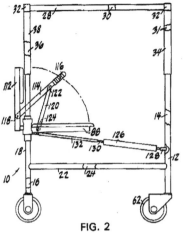

FIG. 2

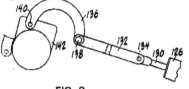

FIG. 8

*Diagrams submitted to the
United States Patent Office,
filed on July 23, 1992.*

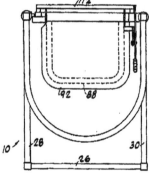

FIG. 1

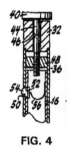

FIG. 4

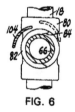

FIG. 6

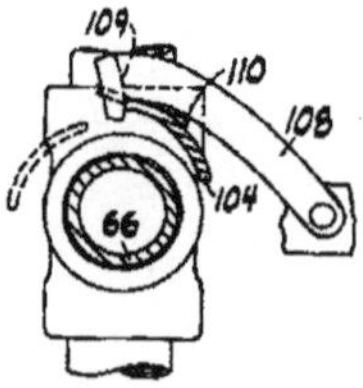

FIG. 7

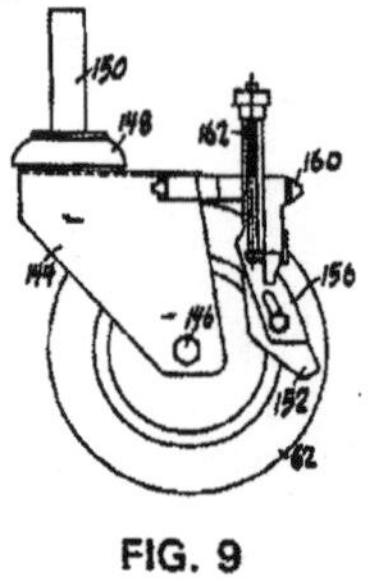

FIG. 9

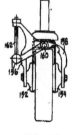

FIG. 10

230

US PATENT

Patent Number: 5,224,721
Date of Patent: July 6, 1993
WALKER HAVING FOLDING AND PIVOTING SEAT APPARATUS
Filed: Jul. 23, 1992
Inventor: Theresa M. Santmann

In the years of the early 1990s the standard procedure during a patient's recovery period from a broken hip left many patients bedridden for a many days.

I was walking in a hospital hallway and noticed a circular piece of metal on the floor of an alcove when a thought came to me, what if a circular piece of metal could be raised on adjustable four metal legs with wheels on two legs enabling rotation of the unit to provide a patient arm support while standing in an upright position?

Later on special features were added including an opening and closing into the unit, a seat that could be lowered for a rest period and raised while walking, and a support harness that would be worn like a diaper and fastened to the framework if needed for security against falling.

There were three units that reached full production with one being given away. The end result was the unit was too unwieldy for mass production and sale.

A CHASTENING CHASE

By Ed Lowe, 1994

As the executive director and owner of a nursing home Terri Santmann periodically attended seminars on a variety of subjects related to the care and comfort of residents who already had lived considerably longer than she. Her preferred mode of transportation to and from these educational meetings was her automobile, which—due to both her schedule and her temperament—she often operated at speeds exceeding the locally posted limits.

One afternoon following a seminar at Mercy Medical Center in Rockville Center, Santmann began driving eastbound on the Southern State Parkway, and at a brisk pace, when she found herself in the left lane behind a blue car operated by a man too satisfied with his leisurely pace for Santmann's impatient taste. Accordingly, she transferred to the center lane and accelerated until she had passed the blue sedan. She would have returned then to the left lane, ahead of the blue car, but the blue car suddenly accelerated as if to keep pace with her, with the result that the space she had intended to occupy in the left lane, in front of the blue car, was now occupied by the blue car.

Santmann might have been satisfied to speed along in tandem with the blue car but for the aggressive gestures she thought she saw in her periphery. She could not be certain without turning to her left to look, but she half-imagined she had seen the operator of the blue car raise his arm at least once in a rapid and therefore seemingly violent gesticulation. She felt as if she looked directly at him and confirmed her fears; the gestures would only intensify, making the drive insufferably uncomfortable at the very least. So, she did not look but instead accelerated again, much more suddenly. Operating now at a rate of speed higher even than she had originally intended, Santmann flipped on her left directional signal and simultaneously turned the wheel, changing lanes and occupying the space she previously had planned to arrange for herself in the left lane, ahead of the blue car, whose operator she clearly had surprised.

A quick glance in the rear-view mirror showed the blue car's driver smacking his forehead with the heel of his right hand in what Santmann considered to be an excessively melodramatic gesture of exasperation. It did serve to indicate without doubt, however, that she had displeased him. Santmann hoped that he would have the self-confidence and fortitude to simply continue on his way and forget about it.

He did not. From the way the grill of the blue car rose in Santmann's rear-view mirror, she deduced that the driver had gunned his accelerator. He next switched race-car like into the lane Santmann only recently had abandoned. He roared ahead until he was adjacent to Santmann's car. She steadfastly refused to look at him, and he roared ahead again, gesturing animatedly, then dropping back to ride alongside her, then roaring ahead and waving some more. Her peripheral vision caught several characteristics of his gestures, but she could not turn her head to solve the mystery of their meaning. Her heart pounding she stared straight ahead, until the car in front of her had proceeded far enough ahead of the car traveling adjacent to it for Santmann to speed up, cut right, speed up again and return to the left lane, leaving the blue car trapped behind in traffic.

The maneuver infuriated the driver of the blue car. He promptly repeated Santmann's actions with an enthusiasm perilously close to vengeful. Glancing up fitfully at her mirror, Santmann thought she could see the man waving either his fist or four-fifths of his fist, and she decided that she would devote the rest of her drive to Babylon to losing him. He entertained an opposite goal. The chase thus proceeded through central and eastern Nassau County, into Suffolk County, where a now-terrified Santmann devised a series of alternate schemes to lure her tormentor into a police precinct or at the very least a crowded service station having convinced herself that he was a homicidal maniac or ... gasp ... worse. If he followed her onto the ramp of the southbound exit for Route 109, she thought that he was a murderer, and she was a goner.

Her heart sank when he did. She decided to pass the First Precinct of the Suffolk County Police, because she would have to make a U-turn to get to it, and she saw no officers outside. Closer to Babylon, with a school building on her right at a fork in the road ahead,

She roared left into the service station, jumped out of her car and ran out into the oncoming lane of traffic, waving and screaming for assistance from passersby. The blue car roared in behind Santmann's car. "Please help me!" Santmann wailed to a northbound man who slowed down and opened his window. "I'm being chased by a madman!"

The northbound man looked over Santmann's shoulder, and the change that so drastically altered his expression inspired Santmann to look back, herself. She spied a man wearing a Nassau County police uniform, storming toward her, waving wildly and yelling in the most convincingly emphatic terms that he was determined to devote the rest of his life to making that Santmann would never be allowed to operate a motor vehicle so long as innocent, sane people inhabited the same planet. Caught somewhere between terror, realization, relief and indignation, Santmann shouted back, "You! I thought you were a murderer!"

While the enraged officer copied down the information from Santmann's license and registration, a now-enraged Santmann strode to the rear of the officer's personal vehicle and copied down his license plate number. The gesture seemed to have a sobering effect on the officer, and the two exchanged calmer, though still diametrically opposite, evaluations of each other's behavior. He called her a maniac. She called him a pervert.

Trembling visibly, and with increasing intensity as she at once recovered and realized how frightened she had been, Santmann folded her arms and said to the officer, "Look, why don't you just give me a cigarette and let me go home." For some reason, he did just that.

ANNA DINI

Anna Dini was an employee at Little Flower Residence in the 1970s, 1980s, and 1990s. The following eulogy was read at the altar of St. Joseph's Church in Babylon by Theresa Santmann at the funeral Mass for Anna Dini:

May 26, 1994

Sometimes you are fortunate enough to meet someone who unfailingly thinks of other people first. Anna Dini was one of those people. She was concerned for all who surrounded her. She was the gentle one who brought my two-year-old to the park to feed the ducks. She was the protector of her patients. She guarded their well-being in a physical sense and also in a spiritual sense. Her family was always in her thoughts and in her prayers. There was never a time when she didn't give the extra touch, the extra helping hand, the concern, the love that was her wont.

I shall love her always.

Anna
By Theresa Santmann

Anna Dini on any day was happy
Kind in every way
She lived her life with trust and grace
A ready smile upon her face

For thirty years and over
This friend and I grew near

Always ready with some kind word
She daily spread some cheer
And as her days were drawing close
She felt God's presence near

Then at her time of ending
A smile crowned her face
As this lovely caring woman
Left her life with ease and grace.

Good-bye, my friend. God bless you.

LITTLE FLOWER NURSING

East Islip, New York   December 1985

To Mrs. Santmann

For the New Year, we have ordered the following for you:

1. Dietary Department will forever more run smoothly. They will have a "Change of Heart," come to work every day and have it spotlessly clean.
2. Nursing will stop replacing who replaces, who replaces, who, etc.
3. Long Beach will cut all bills to the Nursing Home by at least 50%
4. 75% Private pay patients and residents.
5. All payments and Social Security checks will come in on time automatically.
6. Stan Isreal will be sent to Siberia.
7. Jake Springhorn will join him.
8. The "Wind" will blow in the right direction, without any help from you.
9. Your "Alveoli" will become immune to our cigarette smoke.
10. The Hines Commission will fade into oblivion.
11. Mrs. Wong will be sent to Bermuda forever.
12. Terry promises to pay you every Friday!! (That took a lot of doing)
13. The Hero Hut will never run out of Sausage Heroes.
14. Last but not least—A VERY HEALTHY AND HAPPY NEW YEAR.

Affectionately, Your "CRAZY" Office Crew

August 27, 1985

Dear Rose,

This time of year with your and my birthdays only one week apart and our being the same age for one week is always a period of fond recollections for me. You sent such a lovely card;
I was sorry to miss the reunion.
Some of my fondest memories are of you and me.
You never ratted on me no matter what you heard or saw.
You were always loyal.
You were fun and always gave me such a measure of assurance I didn't get from anyone else.
You always had a smile.
You were always kind and thoughtful.

Lots of Love to Someone Special
Terry

Theresa Patnode Santmann enjoying the 2012 Medalist Ceremony.

ELLIS ISLAND MEDAL OF HONOR

Theresa Patnode Santmann
2012 Medalist

Theresa Patnode Santmann started life in humble surroundings, growing up on a farm in upstate New York. She began her professional career as a registered nurse, and through hard work and determination, Santmann became a highly successful entrepreneur, inventor and business woman. She was the founder and executive director of two nursing homes in Suffolk County, Little Flower Nursing and Rehabilitation in East Islip and Petite Fleur Nursing Home in Sayville. Additionally she created "In Katie's Care" a respite center, named for her granddaughter, for the Suffolk County Girl Scouts Council.

Philanthropically, the personal commitment and generosity of Theresa Santmann has reverberated throughout Long Island including a $1,000,000 gift in support of Winthrop University Hospital's innovative research program. This contribution is aimed at finding the cause and a cure for Amyotrophic Lateral Sclerosis (ALS) known as Lou Gehrig's disease. Santmann's interest in research resulted when her late husband, John, was diagnosed with the disease at the age of 30 and succumbed to the illness 18 years later.

In the year of 2011 President Keen of Farmingdale College announced the largest gift in the history of the college, $1,000,000 donated by Theresa Patnode Santmann. The gift is creating four scholarships spread over the program in nursing, bioscience, dental hygiene and medical technology and will support faculty research and the enhancing of student research.

Theresa Santmann is also active in her community, having served as the president of the Babylon Village School Board, president of the Babylon Village Chamber of Commerce and president of the

Babylon Village Youth Project. Currently she serves as vice president of Splashes of Hope.

Over the years Theresa Santmann has received many awards for her humanitarian efforts. In 1998, she was honored for the March of Dimes Woman of Distinction. In 1999, she received an honorary Doctor of Science degree and a Distinguished Citizen Award from Dowling College. Having been named one of Long Island's top 50 women three times, she was inducted into the "Hall of Fame" by Long Island Business News. In 2006 she was honored by the Suffolk County Clerk and the law firm Siben and Siben at a fund raiser to benefit Hospice Care Network.

Theresa Santmann's accomplishments are multiple and diverse, including a published autobiography entitled, *In Gratitude to My Guardian Angel.* In 1993, in an effort to make the patients in her nursing homes more comfortable she developed a walker with a folding, pivoting seat and harness, for which she holds a patent.

From 1998 to the present she has sponsored 37 students in order for them to attend St. Lukes School in the Bronx.

NEW YORK STATE ASSEMBLY CITATION

In Recognition of Distinguished Honoree

WHEREAS, Theresa Patnode Santmann is so deservedly honored by Splashes of Hope for her dedication and service at the Annual Gala & Art Auction held at Land's End Restaurant in Sayville, New York; and

WHEREAS, The heart of any community is found in outstanding and unique people, who through commitment to others, generosity of spirit and dedication to purpose, serve as an inspiration to our community; and

WHEREAS, Theresa Patnode Santmann received her nursing degree from Farmingdale State in 1969, a few years after purchasing a rental property in Babylon, which she converted into an adult home. Her late husband John, was diagnosed with Lou Gehrig's disease and was her first patient. She later built and operated Little Flower Nursing Home in East Islip and Petite Fleur Nursing Home in Sayville. In 1993, Santmann invented and patented a walker with a folding, pivoting seat. She has used knowledge and opportunity to give back to those in need of help, and her charitable work is something which should be emulated by all; and

WHEREAS, Founded in 1996 by Heather Buggee, Splashes of Hope works with volunteer artists, to bring murals to hospitals, children's centers, and as many other facilities as possible. Through the support of dedicated members like Theresa Splashes of Hope has been able to grow into an international organization, receiving mural requests from facilities throughout the United States and the world. Since its inception, over 200 volunteers have helped make Heather's vision of colorful and comforting hospital interior's a reality; and

WHEREAS, Theresa Patnode Santmann has been a leader during her service as the Vice President of Splashes of Hope, she has worked as a sponsor of the Northport Veterans Affairs Splashes of Hope Project, which designed a beautiful beach mural at the Northport Veterans Affairs Medical Center and has provided aesthetically pleasing environments for the brave men who have served our country. Now, Therefore Be It

RESOLVED, That I, Andrew P. Raia, as duly elected Member of the State Assembly of New York and on behalf of the residents of the Twelfth District, on this Twelfth Day of April in the year Two Thousand Thirteen, hereby congratulate and commend

THERESA PATNODE SANTMANN

As an individual who is worthy of the esteem of the community and the Great State of New York

Assemblyman Andrew P. Raia

CHRISTMAS COMES EARLY TO THE RIDE

Appeared on Facebook, December 24

Chris Pendergast

An afternoon telephone call yesterday jarred my wife and I from our Christmas preparations. On the line was a long time Ride for Life supporter, who has over the years become our friend. The voice announced the news of an extraordinary gift.

Many years ago our friend learned the heartache wrought when a close family member passed away from ALS. The desire to fight the disease has not dissipated, despite the passing of time. When our benefactor discovered the Ride For Life, an outlet was presented to even the score against ALS. We have enjoyed generous support from our friend. However, this Holiday Season was to be different.

I heard my wife exclaiming something and talking into the phone excitedly. Preoccupied with Holiday thoughts, my attention drifted away. The next thing I realized, she was standing over me with an odd look. Slowly she began saying, "We just got a Christmas gift for the Ride." I asked her what she was talking about and she blurted, "Our friend wants to give us $125,000. They are coming right over right now with the check."

Ordinarily, I no longer enjoy breath taking experiences since ALS has begun paralyzing my respiratory muscles. Understandably, I opt out on anything so thrilling that it promises 'to take your breath away'. However, this gift was an exception. I welcomed it!

When the doorbell rang we opened our door wide and greeted our friend. We sat around the kitchen table and shared a glass of Bailey's Irish Cream. We dreamed of the New Year, the research that we can fund and toasted to the day our world will be free from ALS.

Our friend wishes to remain in the background. Respectfully, I am posting this story and anonymously referring to our benefactor, This Holiday; remember the true spirit of the season: giving.

Thank you, friend.

*Picture of
Theresa
taken by a
friend off the
south shore
of Long Island,
New York,
1992.*

Chapter 40

Keep Me in a Pocket
Next to Your Heart

The following is a message from the twentieth century to you of the twenty-first century:

The last century has brought mind-boggling changes in our lifestyles and in our medical and scientific advancements, as well as in our expectations, even though the mechanical workings of our bodies have not changed.

When you hear of either how good or how bad anything has been in the history of humankind, please take heart. Your psychological, intellectual, and bodily responses are very similar to mine. Your fears, your loves, and your hates all make us as one with the very earth that nurtures us. Go forward with dignity and courage.

You may land on the moon; plant a flower in my name. You may fly; carry me on your wings. You may explore the ocean depths; leave a little space in your subterranean vehicle. You may explore the North Pole; keep me in a pocket next to your heart.

I am your past—your grandmother, your grandfather, and your ancestors in every sense. I breathe the same air. I feel the same soil and swim the same oceans.

I have carried you, and now is the time for you to carry me.

God bless.